Tropical Forested Watersheds

Westview Replica Editions

The concept of Westview Replica Editions is a response to the continuing crisis in academic and informational publishing. Library budgets for books have been severely curtailed. Ever larger portions of general library budgets are being diverted from the purchase of books and used for data banks, computers, micromedia, and other methods of information retrieval. Interlibrary loan structures further reduce the edition sizes required to satisfy the needs of the scholarly community. Economic pressures on the university presses and the few private scholarly publishing companies have severely limited the capacity of the industry to properly serve the academic and research communities. As a result, many manuscripts dealing with important subjects, often representing the highest level of scholarship, are no longer economically viable publishing projects—or, if accepted for publication, are typically subject to lead times ranging from one to three years.

Westview Replica Editions are our practical solution to the problem. We accept a manuscript in camera-ready form, typed according to our specifications, and move it immediately into the production process. As always, the selection criteria include the importance of the subject, the work's contribution to scholarship, and its insight, originality of thought, and excellence of exposition. The responsibility for editing and proofreading lies with the author or sponsoring institution. We prepare chapter headings and display pages, file for copyright, and obtain Library of Congress Cataloging in Publication Data. A detailed manual contains simple instructions for preparing the final typescript, and our editorial staff is always available to answer questions.

The end result is a book printed on acid-free paper and bound in sturdy library-quality soft covers. We manufacture these books ourselves using equipment that does not require a lengthy make-ready process and that allows us to publish first editions of 300 to 600 copies and to reprint even smaller quantities as needed. Thus, we can produce Replica Editions quickly and can keep even very specialized books in print as long as there is a demand for them.

About the Book and Authors

Tropical Forested Watersheds: Hydrologic and Soils Response to Major Uses or Conversions
by Lawrence S. Hamilton with Peter N. King

Tropical forests are being altered or replaced at a rate that has aroused much concern among the global scientific community. Of particular importance is the effect on soil and water of activities involving alterations and conversions of forests for cultivation, grazing, logging or other purposes. This book synthesizes current knowledge about the effects of twelve different human activities on various water and soil phenomena, including groundwater, spring, and well levels; streamflow quantity, timing and distribution; on-site erosion; sediment in streams; and nutrient outflow. Each chapter includes a short section suggesting appropriate management and policy guidelines to minimize adverse effects and enhance benefits.

Lawrence S. Hamilton is a Research Associate with the East-West Environment and Policy Institute of the East-West Center, Honolulu, Hawaii, U.S.A.

Peter N. King is an associate with ACIL Agricultural Consultants, Melbourne, Australia. He was a visiting Research Fellow at the East-West Environment and Policy Institute from December 1981 to May 1982.

The following participants at a Watershed Forest Influence Workshop collaborated on this book: Johari Baharudin, Michael Bonell, F. Herbert Bormann, Walter Boughton, David Cassells, Kasem Chunkao, James Douglass, Peter Drysdale, Samir El-Swaify, Lawrence Hamilton, Yuan-lin Lin, Low Kwai Sim, Syafii Manan, Harley Manner, Walter Megahan, Colin O'Loughlin, Jemuel Perino, Samarn Rouysungnern, Severo Saplaco, Yoshinori Tsukamoto, Napoleon Vergara, Les Whitmore, Hulton Wood, Frank Zadroga.

This book was published with the assistance of a grant to the East-West Environment and Policy Institute by UNESCO's Man and the Biosphere Program (MAB), through the Division of Ecological Sciences, Paris, France.

Tropical Forested Watersheds
Hydrologic and Soils Response to Major Uses or Conversions

by Lawrence S. Hamilton
with Peter N. King

Westview Press / Boulder, Colorado

A Westview Replica Edition

Published in 1983 in the United States of America by
  Westview Press, Inc.
  5500 Central Avenue
  Boulder, Colorado 80301
  Frederick A. Praeger, President and Publisher

Library of Congress Catalog Card Number: 83-50068
ISBN 0–86531–994–4

Printed and bound in the United States of America

10   9   8   7   6   5

CONTENTS

Preface

In attempting this state-of-knowledge synthesis on tropical forest influences and effects of forest alterations, the workshop participants and the author were dismayed at the paucity of reliable data. It was therefore necessary to rely to some extent on professional judgments based on information from small plots and short time periods. Sorely needed are more studies on entire small- and medium-size watersheds having measuring weirs or flumes and good instrumentation, with periods of calibration and records over periods of 5 to 25 years. Such long-term experiments are extremely rare in the developing countries where most of the world's tropical forests are found. Sir Charles Pereira has pointed out that four such experimental catchments were begun in the decade 1955–65 in East Africa, West Africa, Indonesia, and India. Unfortunately those in West Africa and Indonesia succumbed to the stresses of the transition to independence. Fortunately, some excellent work has been initiated in the 1970s in Australia's tropics and subtropics, and within the past two years, some complete watershed studies have been installed in Malaysia. A recent watershed installation in Taiwan is shown in Figure 1.

It was therefore necessary to fall back at times on research results from temperate zone watersheds (Coweeta, United States; Kamabuchi, Japan; Melbourne Water Supply, Australia; etc.) and to suggest that the hydrologic processes should not be different. Again, professional judgments are required and were made in order that the ultimate objective be realized, namely, providing information to those making land-use policies for tropical watersheds. It is our opinion that too many of the land-use policies for tropical uplands are being made on the basis of misinformation and mythology and that imperfect information is being used in cases where there is more information available. For this reason, each chapter is concluded with a summary that attempts to put the forest land-use activity and its effects into a form that speaks to policymakers.

Grateful acknowledgment is rendered to the workshop participants, who provided much of the material for this report and reviewed the manuscript. Their names and affiliations are listed in Appendix A. When spe-

Figure 1. Watershed 3 in warm temperate rainforest at Lien-Hua-Chi, Taiwan, installed by Taiwan Forest Research Institute (3.4 ha, 69-percent slope).

cific unpublished information is attributed to one of them, it is cited in the text as personal communication (e.g. "Manan 1981, Pers. Comm.").

Special thanks also to Peter King who helped synthesize this material in its early stages and who provided his own expertise. I acknowledge members of the East-West Center Publications Office staff for their contributions toward bringing this book to its published form.

I also acknowledge the assistance of UNESCO's Man and the Biosphere (MAB) Program in providing funds to assist in publication of this synthesis. In particular, Dr. Leo Teller of UNESCO/MAB has been helpful both in the logistics and in the technical review of the manuscript.

This synthesis and activity is part of a larger project on watershed land use being conducted as part of a program area in Human Interactions with Tropical Ecosystems at the East-West Environment and Policy Institute.

Lawrence S. Hamilton

Introduction

THE RESEARCH PROBLEM

Tropical forests are different from temperate forests. But are they so different in their hydrological functions, their role in protecting soils from erosion, or in their nutrient cycling that they respond quite differently when "disturbed" or converted to other uses? Most scientific evidence indicates that differences are "more in degree than in kind." Conventional wisdom, political statements, and land-use policy formulation would, however, all seem to indicate that the situation is markedly different.

For instance, a 1981 issue of *World Water* carried an article about India's Chipko (tree hugging movement), which originated in the state of Uttar Pradesh. It suggested that trees can prevent monsoonal floods and subsequent droughts, and quotes the movement's leader as saying, "Tree-planting particularly of broadleaved varieties creates water" (*World Water* 1981). Research results from several temperate watershed research stations give quite different findings. They show that trees generally use more water than do lower forms of vegetation, particularly on deep soils, and that tree planting generally results in reduced total water yields from catchments. There have been no experimental findings showing increased rainfall following afforestation.

As far as floods are concerned, experimental evidence from temperate areas shows that small storm peakflows and upstream flooding on small streams are reduced following afforestation. For major storms in large watersheds, afforestation or deforestation had only a minor impact on flood peaks and duration. Again, this has not stopped statements to the contrary. In early 1981 when Philippine newspapers carried graphic accounts of the repeated and disastrous Agusan River floods, a political leader blamed "denudation of the forests by logging as responsible for about 30% of the flooding" (Corvera 1981). Even though flooding is an annual event, this particular flood was given a return period of 20 years. Furthermore, Openshaw (1974) has stated, "The principal cause of the recent floods in the Indian subcontinent was the removal of tree cover in the catchment areas for fuelwood (and shifting cultivation)." The section of this report on Harvesting Fuelwood and Lopping Fodder deals with the effects of fuelwood cutting on water, and this is preceded by a section on the effects of shifting agriculture. There seems to be little evidence supporting Openshaw's unqualified statement, though the impacts of long-term, large-scale land abuse have indeed not been researched.

Elsewhere in the tropics, afforestation is being recommended as official government policy in order to rejuvenate springs and small streams. It is being suggested that *Imperata* and *Themeda* grasslands be planted with trees to increase dry season flows so that there is more water available for irrigation. Research on several temperate experimental watersheds would lead one to question whether this objective can be met solely through afforestation. In fact, most available research evidence suggests lower dry season flows following conversion to forest.

Other forest watershed policies being promulgated and implemented in developing countries effectively close the forest to many forms of human use. For instance, total bans on logging and shifting cultivation have been incorporated into some national policies, although they are frequently impossible to implement. Is total exclusion of human activity really necessary to protect the desirable hydrologic functions of watersheds? Experience and research in temperate forests would indicate that controlled and managed use may be a better policy for maximizing net social benefits.

Are the processes so different in tropical versus temperate watersheds that different policies and land management strategies are required? It is well established that the infiltration, storage, and release of water; the detachment, transport, and deposition of soil particles; and the cycling of nutrients depend on complex interactions between topography, climate, soil, geology, vegetation, and human manipulation of natural systems. There is no intrinsic reason why tropical systems should respond to different laws of nature than do temperate ones. Yet it must be recognized that both the nature of the driving variables (e.g., precipitation intensity or temperature) and the response of a system (e.g., sediment yield or evapotranspiration loss) may be quite different in the tropics.

As watershed experiments are generally long-term, expensive, and require a high degree of technical competence, most research evidence to date comes from the temperate, industrialized countries. Direct extrapolation of results to different combinations of climate, soil, and vegetation, even within the temperate zone, always has been problematical, so we should not be surprised that direct transfer of research to an entirely different climatic zone is fraught with uncertainty. There is no reason to believe that the basic processes are different. The research to prove it, however, must be carried out under a wide range of conditions so that a set of generalizations can be made for the range of conditions that exist in the tropics.

Possibly the kind and degree of forest disturbance in the tropics is also important. If there are different hydrologic, soil movement, and nutrient cycling responses, it might be due to differences in the nature of the impactor. For instance, there may not be an analog for swiddening or kaingin in the temperate forest experiments. The "mountain farming" experiment at Coweeta Hydrologic Laboratory in North Carolina (Dils 1953) is not analogous to slash-and-burn agriculture. Can evidence from tractor logging experiments be used to assess the impact of teak logging using elephants in Thailand?

Di Castri and Hadley (1979) have identified some of the problems in using research data to solve important applied problems in the tropical developing countries. They pointed out that much of the research is concentrated in temperate industrialized countries, that information from such research may not be transferable, and that the extent of the transferability is unknown. Their typology of information transfer and use problems and the underlying causes is so clearly relevant to watershed forest influences that it is reproduced in Table 1.

In watershed forest influences, there is certainly an uneven geographic coverage of research and inadequate use and application of data, but the real question relates to the applicability, especially when trying to transfer data from specific experiments in temperate watersheds to applied problems in tropical watersheds. On many occasions, it has proved difficult enough to extend the results from small temperate area watersheds to large watersheds in another area of the same state or country. It is undoubtedly even more difficult to extend the research from small watershed experiments in temperate countries to applied problems in tropical countries.

EAST-WEST CENTER WATERSHED FOREST INFLUENCES WORKSHOP

To assess the state of knowledge of tropical watershed forest influences research and the possible use of information from temperate watershed research, a workshop was convened in late September 1981 at the East-West Center's Environment and Policy Institute, bringing together the active and outstanding forest hydrology researchers of the Asian-Pacific region. Twenty-six participants and invited observers from 12 countries were able to attend and to address these problems (see Appendix A). By-products of the workshop are a 250-page selected annotated bibliography of tropical watershed research (Williams and Hamilton 1982) and a compilation of status reports on watershed research from 11 countries and Hawaii (Hamilton and Bonell 1982).

The principal task, however, was to synthesize what is known about the role of forests as watershed cover in the tropics and how that role changes as the forest is used or converted to other uses. The six impacts considered were changes in groundwater, springs, and wells; streamflow quantity (an-

Table 1. Research Information Transfer and Use Problems

Main Problems	Main Causes
Uneven geographic coverage and incompleteness of information	
	• Research concentrated in temperate industrialized countries
	• Current policies do not stimulate creation of new knowledge in developing countries
	• Present trends do not favor research in some fields (e.g., taxonomy of tropical plants and animals)
Inadequate use and application of data	
	• Data not widely available
	• Data presented in a form not understandable to planners and local populations
Lack of applicability of data (or data leading to unpredictable or adverse effects when applied)	
	• Data lack relevance to, or adequacy in facing, specific situations
	• Data result from research that is overly sectoral and incompatible with complexity of situations
	• Data take little account of people's different perceptions of a given problem or situation
	• Site data cannot be extrapolated for regional and national planning purposes within a country
	• Data not transferable between countries, or extent of transferability unknown.

Source: Adapted from di Castri and Hadley (1979).

nual water yield); timing and distribution of streamflow; on-site erosion; sediment in streams; and nutrient outflow in stream water.

Since the ultimate objective is to use this information in planning and policymaking, a series of uses and transformations that commonly occur in tropical developing countries was set forth. A matrix of causes and effects (Table 2) was used as the organizational framework for the workshop.

Prior to the workshop, each participant was asked to indicate the information available to him or her for each of the cells of the matrix and to classify the information as follows:

Class I   — First-hand research evidence
Class II   — Authoritative literature references
Class III — Professional judgment or empirical observation and conventional or folk wisdom that has not been disproved
        0 — No information

Each participant then brought to the workshop the available information keyed to these cells. The workshop discussions focused in turn on each of these interactions, thus bringing out the collective wisdom and experience of the researchers on the effects of each use or transformation of the forest. Table 2 shows the matrix filled in for a hypothetical knowledge situation in one country.

Some additional questions also were considered: The role of cloud forest in water capture and what happens to this "occult" precipitation when the forest is removed, differences in the hydrologic roles of pure plantations versus mixed forests and broadleaved versus coniferous forests, and the criteria for delineating critical watershed areas. Finally, some attention was given to logging guidelines for important watershed forests.

This state-of-knowledge synthesis is organized into sections according to type of forest use or conversion (the actions). Each section first describes and delineates the activity, and then discusses what is known or believed about the effects of that activity on the six water and soil parameters considered. (The nutrient outflow section does not deal with biological water quality, nor does it deal with nutrient export from the site due to removal of biomass.) We then attempt in the summary to discuss the forest-land planning and management strategies that take cognizance of this forest influence information and judgment. Policy decisions about land use must be made even when our knowledge in the arena of watershed forest influences is imperfect.

Table 2. Information Matrix — Watershed Forest Use or Conversions

		A	B	C	D	E	F
				Change in			
Effect of these actions ↓	On these phenomena →	Water Table, Springs, or Wells	Water Quantity in Stream over year	Water Timing of Stream Discharge	Erosion Rate on Site	Sediment in Stream	Nutrient Input into Stream
Effect of these uses of forests	1. Minor forest product uses (gathering, tapping, etc., no tree cutting)	III	III	III	III	III	III
	2. Stable shifting agriculture (fallow sufficiently long that system is sustained)	0	I	I	II	II	0
	3. Fuelwood harvesting (no roading or vehicles) and fodder lopping	0	0	0	0	0	0
	4. Commercial wood harvesting a) commonly used logging practices	III	I; II	I; II	I	I	II
	b) Improved watershed protection logging	0	II	II	III	III	II
	5. Grazing on forestland	0	0	0	II	II	0
	6. Burning forestland	0	0	0	0	0	0
Effects of these conversions	7. To forest tree plantations	III	0	0	0	0	0
	8. To grassland/savanna for grazing (and/or burned to maintain)	III	II	II	II	0	0
	9. To food or extractive tree crop plantations (e.g., coffee, tea, rubber, oil palm, banana)	0	II	II	II	II	I; II
	10. To annual cropping a) without terracing, contours, etc.	III	III	III	III	III	III
	b) with soil conservation practices	0	0	0	0	0	0
	11. To agroforestry a) Tree crops with grazing	0	0	0	0	0	0
	b) Tree crops with annual crops	0	0	III	III	0	0
Effects of	12. Reforestation or afforestation	III	II	II	I	I	0
	13. Other						

Class I — first-hand research evidence
Class II — authoritative literature references
Class III — professional judgment
0 — no information

1
Harvesting Minor Forest Products

In many developing countries, minor forest products provide much of the requirement for food, tools, and shelter (i.e., subsistence) of people dwelling in or near forests. In addition, minor forest products may provide the raw materials for small-scale cottage industries and thus are important to local economies. These products are usually gathered or hunted in wild forests, though some management of vegetation or animals may be involved.

Normally, the impact on the forest ecosystem is a small one, and a type of sustained yield system prevails. Some examples of minor forest product use include harvesting of foods (wild yams, bamboo shoots, fruits and nuts), medicinal plants, poisonous plants, woody lianas and other rope-like climbers, and leaves and twigs for wrapping food or thatching; collecting various plant parts for tanning or dyeing; cutting rattan for making baskets and furniture; tapping for resins and turpentine; gathering wild honey or using forest tree flowers for apiary purposes; hunting or capturing wildlife for food and ornamentation, and for skins to be used as clothing, shelter, or utensils; and removal of forest litter for various uses. Table 3 illustrates the range of uses of forest plants in Papua New Guinea (Lea 1975).

Table 3. Minor Forest Product Uses in Papua New Guinea

Use	Example
Abortificants and contraceptives	*Caldesia parnassitolia*
Artifacts	"Galip nuts" for tourists, wood in masks, shields, etc.
Bark cloth	Beaten *Ficus* sp. for "tapa" cloth
Basketwork	*Kygodium* sp.
Beverages	Palm wine, sap from vines and creepers
Bird bait	*Melanolepis multiglandulosa* fruit attracts cockatoos
Condiments	*Zingiber* sp., *Amomum* sp.
Containers	Bamboo and gourds for carrying water

Cooking and eating utensils	"Kwila" bowls (*Intsia bijuga*), bamboo stems and coconut shells
Decoration and ornaments	Seeds of *Coix lacryma-jobi* in necklaces and leaves of *Celosia* and *Olearia*
Drugs	*Areca* nuts
Dyes	*Bixa orellana* (red), *Curcuma longa* (yellow), *Leucosyke* (black)
Exudates	Guttapercha (rubber)
Fibers	*Gnetum gnemon* and *Althoffia pleiostigma* for net bags
Fish intoxicants	*Derris*
Food	Many species
Glazing	*Celtis* for glazing black paint among the Abelam
Gums	*Artocarpus* for caulking and bird traps
Insecticides	*Pyrethrum*
Juices and saps	Toddies and stimulants such as *Anamirta* and "kava" (*Piper methysticum*)
Medicines	Many species
Musical instruments	*Pterocarpus indicus* for "kundus" and *Vitex coffassus* for "garamuts"
Oils	Tree oil from *Campnosperma* and *Pandanus* oil seed
Poisons	*Derris, Gnetum catifolium*
Resins	*Parinari* (the kusta nut)
"Rope"	*Calamus* for "kanda" and *Lygodium* for weaving masks and baskets
Salt making	*Coix gigantea* among the Baruya and *Eriocaulon longifolium*
Starch	*Sago, Manihot* and *Tacca* spp.
Thatching	*Sago* and *Nipa* fronds and "kunai" grass (*Imperata* and *Miscanthus* in the highlands)
Tool making	*Bambusa* stems, *Diospyros* wood
Wearing apparel	*Pandanus* leaf capes and penis gourds
Weapon making	*Caryota* for bows

Source: Adapted from Lea (1975).

Some uses listed above and in Table 3 involve cutting down trees, but for our purposes we define the activity of harvesting minor forest products as that involving no significant cutting of trees. If trees are cut, the impacts

Table 4. Effects of Litter Removal on Infiltration Capacity

Soil Horizon	Untreated Infiltration Rate (mm/min)	Treated Infiltration Rate (mm/min)
H	120	2
A$_1$	60	0
A$_2$	14	4
B	5	3

Source: Tsukamoto (1975).

become more akin to fuelwood harvesting or commercial wood harvesting. Even so, in some places the intensity of use may become so great (often due to the development of a cash commodity value or a village industry) that the forest resource base is damaged (as in excessive resin tapping) or the product is overharvested and becomes scarce. The latter has happened and is happening in the case of rattan in several parts of Asia. In the Philippines, the Ministry of Natural Resources has had to ban rattan harvesting in all experimental forests, national parks, wilderness areas, and any special areas where problems exist (Anonymous 1980). Moreover, it has encouraged rattan planting and sustained yield "rattan farming" by a program of incentives and the production of educational materials on rattan growing (Generalao 1981).

The professional judgment of the workshop participants was that gathering or harvesting of most minor forest products usually has little impact on water yields, timing, erosion rates, sedimentation, and nutrient discharges. There has been no research to support this contention except in a few specific cases in temperate zone forests. A study by Tsukamoto (1975) in Japan provides some information on one particular practice—the removal of forest litter such as might be the case where it is collected either for fuel or for adding organic material to fields. The critical factors are the intensity of use, the degree of soil disturbance, and the nature of the access trails to the gathering sites. In parts of the Himalayan foothills of northern India, for example, overtapping of *Pinus roxburghii* has resulted in windbreak damage and subsequent soil exposure. In the same region, collection of pine litter for a new pressboard-backing industry could cause future problems of erosion and nutrient loss.

GROUNDWATER, SPRINGS, AND WELLS

No direct evidence was produced concerning the effects of minor forest products harvesting on groundwater. However, Tsukamoto's study (1975) on the effects of removing forest litter in Japan shows that infiltration rates decreased markedly for all soil horizons following litter removal (Table 4). These results once again confirm the well-known function of forest litter in holding water temporarily and releasing it gradually to the soil along with dissolved and particulate organic material, which improves the soil structure and infiltration capacity. In the absence of the litter layer, raindrops compact the soil, and infiltration capacity is reduced. When the volume of infiltrating water exceeds the detention capacity of the soil profile on a permeable geologic structure, an increase in groundwater level can be expected. If the removal of litter affects groundwater levels, it would, therefore, seem to cause a decrease.

STREAMFLOW QUANTITY

Tsukamoto (1975) also studied the impact of removing forest litter on streamflow. The experiment was conducted using paired small watersheds at Shirasaka in the Tokyo University Forest in Aichi. All forest litter was removed from the treated watersheds for three consecutive years. Annual discharge was increased by at least 4 percent, mainly due to an increase in direct runoff. For isolated storms of less than 100 mm, the storm hydrographs showed an average 78 percent increase in direct runoff and a 168 percent increase in peak flows. Other minor forest product removal was deemed to have no effect on water yield.

TIMING AND DISTRIBUTION OF STREAMFLOW

Tsukamoto's study indicated the time to peak decrease by 13 percent on the treated area, but there was no change in time to end of direct runoff. Apart from this study, the workshop participants cited no other evidence about the impact of harvesting minor forest products on the storm hydrograph. However, they agreed that the effects were likely to be minor.

ON-SITE EROSION

Most of the evidence suggests that the harvesting of most minor forest products will not cause serious soil erosion. Complete litter removal, as practiced in parts of China in the recent past, is certainly one exception. In Tsukamoto's (1975) study, however, only small amounts of soil erosion were observed, and this was attributed to effective surface protection by a dense, concentrated network of fine roots. Over three years, splash erosion was serious, and on one-third of the watershed, all of the H layer had disappeared.

The heavy use of forest trails may result in soil compaction, increased surface runoff, and then gullying. This certainly has been documented in the case of heavily used recreational hiking trails in North America. The effects in tropical developing countries will obviously depend on traffic volume, soil characteristics, and rainfall intensity. Trails through forests in montane Papua New Guinea have eroded and are sources of sediment (Manner 1981, Pers. Comm.).

In Fiji, harvesting of reeds and bamboo for rafts, thatching, and building material is thought to have had localized but relatively minor impacts on stream-bank erosion due to soil disturbance at the harvesting site.

SEDIMENT IN STREAMS

There is no evidence that minor forest products harvesting causes serious stream sedimentation problems, and workshop participants agreed that only minor impacts could be expected from trails and stream crossings as mentioned previously.

NUTRIENT OUTFLOW

There was no evidence presented on nutrient outflows caused by minor forest products harvesting in the region. However, it is known that nutrient depletion through continual long-term gathering of forest litter occurred in temperate forests in Germany and the practice had to be controlled. Similar effects plus erosion were reported in the Republic of Korea, where the Forest Law of 1973 prohibited leaf raking and removal of grass litter within forest areas. It is not thought that these practices would change the nutrient contents of streams to any significant extent.

SUMMARY AND IMPLICATIONS

The continuation or expansion of minor forest products harvesting is unlikely to have a major detrimental impact on any of the watershed variables considered. However, in the case of high-quality, untreated water supply areas, some level of intensity can lead to water quality problems (sediment or disease contamination). Removal of forest litter for fuel or for use on fields can result in accelerated erosion, sedimentation, and loss of nutrients and organic matter from the site, and should be controlled.

2
Shifting Agriculture

Shifting agriculture (usually cultivation, but sometimes grazing) forms a continuum from extensive (sustainable) to intensive (unstable) uses of land, depending on the length of the fallow period (Clarke 1966). In various places this activity is called swidden, kaingin, conuco, slash-and-burn, slash-and-trash, forest fallow, jhum and other local names. Kunstadter and Chapman (1978) describe three kinds of swiddening in northern Thailand: short cultivation/short fallow, short cultivation/long fallow, and long cultivation/very long fallow (or abandonment). Other typologies exist, based on the vegetation (forest, bush savanna, or grassland) and/or the historical background of the practitioners (pioneer-colonist, established, or incipient).

Extensive shifting cultivation systems may be characterized by combinations of:
- Gardening in forest clearings in primary forest or, more commonly, in secondary forest;
- Short periods of cropping alternating with longer periods of forest fallow;
- Low human or animal energy input per unit of energy output (use of fire adds large energy input);
- Use of relatively simple tools;
- Polyculture;
- Low human population density and/or "traditional" people; and
- Little disturbance of the soil surface.

Intensive systems that approach sedentary agriculture may be characterized by combinations of:
- Use of anthropogenic grasslands or degraded bush fallows for gardening or grazing;
- Long periods of cropping alternating with shorter or no periods of fallow;
- High energy input per unit of energy output;
- Use of technically more advanced tools (e.g., chain saws);

- Tendency toward monoculture cash crops;
- High human population density and/or "new colonists"; and
- Greater soil disturbance, which can include rough terracing, ditching, mounding and other edaphic modifications, or use of livestock.

The impact of shifting cultivation on the hydrologic, erosional, and nutrient status of forested watersheds will depend on the position on this continuum of cultivated area, cultivation practices, and crop type (Naprakabob et al. 1975). For the purposes of the workshop and this report, extensive or sustainable shifting agriculture has been chosen as the impactor. In shifting agriculture as we have defined it, it is the fields that shift (rotate), not the people who shift (move on). It is felt that as the frequency and intensity of cultivation increases, the likely effects are akin to those from grazing, annual cropping, or agroforestry (Chapters 8, 10, and 11) in that these land uses are real conversions rather than uses of the forest that maintain a forest most of the time.

Intensive shifting agriculture, for instance, is practiced in tropical grasslands, which already represent a degradation from the original forest condition. This is the "long cultivation/very long fallow" type described by Kunstadter and Chapman (1978). Ultimately, soil fertility is lost, erosion occurs because of relatively deep, clean cultivation with hoes, and the land is abandoned. It returns to degraded forest very slowly and is thus in many ways more akin to conversion to grassland. Its effects are therefore presented in Chapter 8.

One of the best studies of shifting cultivation in the tropics was carried out for FAO in Latin America by Watters (1971). Most of these studies described unstable, intensive systems where the *campesino* "believes that this [felling and burning] is the beginning of agriculture on a permanent basis . . . this type of farmer does not only waste land; he also very often destroys it" (Watters 1971). Shifting cultivation of this type on slopes as steep as 80 or 90 percent is reported from the Venezuelan Andes. Predictably, it results in accelerated sheet and gully erosion of serious proportions.

There are few good experiments showing the effect of stable shifting cultivation within the parameters of concern of this report, nor are there data from temperate zone research that can be transferred with confidence. The mountain agriculture experiments carried out by Dils (1953) and others in the well-known series of studies at the Coweeta Hydrologic Laboratory in humid southeastern North America are scarcely transferable, though they may suggest some general tendencies. In this case, clearing and farming a 9.3 ha forest resulted in over a twelvefold increase in soil loss and sharp increases in storm peaks. However, the Philippines' Forest Research Institute and the College of Forestry, University of the Philippines at Los Banos, are now conducting work pertinent to the tropics.

GROUNDWATER, SPRINGS, AND WELLS

No research on this topic was known to the workshop participants. How-ever, given the nature of extensive, sustainable shifting agricultural land use and its mosaic pattern of small clearings and regrowth, the impact on changing the water table was deemed to be negligible. Surface runoff on plots in the clearings was affected as indicated by Kellman (1969) in Table 5, but there was thought to be no effect on groundwater, springs, and wells.

Table 5. Surface Runoff from Plots with Different Land Use in the Philippines

Plot Location	Sample Period (days)	Surface Runoff as Percent of Precipitation
Primary forest	227	0.258
Softwood tree fallow	227	0.264
Imperata grassland	227	3.017
New abaca plantation	227	0.348
10-year-old abaca plantation	227	0.635
Logged over forest	305	1.73
New corn swidden	138[a]	1.52
	34[b]	
New rice swidden	60[c]	0.86
	158[a]	1.08
	14[b]	
2-year-old corn swidden	60[c]	0.42
	108[a]	1.78
	17[b]	
	19[c]	4.08[e]
	50[d]	0.69
12-year-old corn swidden	125[a]	11.64
	50[d]	6.73
	19[c]	14.15

Source: Adapted from Kellman (1969).

Note: Study was in Mindanao, where annual precipitation averages 422 cm with little seasonal variation. These were small plots (8 m^2) located on 25-percent slope. Period under observation was January to October with the swidden treatments starting in mid-February. These results cannot be extrapolated to watersheds, and the table is presented to serve a qualitative rather than quantitative purpose.

[a]Cropping period.
[b]Intercropping period.
[c]Postcropping period.
[d]Precropping period.
[e]Cleared after harvest.

STREAMFLOW QUANTITY

There seems to be a widely held view influencing land use policy that shifting agriculture is the cause of reduced streamflows. Watters (1971) reported "the drop in river volume that invariably occurs" for the Rio Motatan in Venezuela from 1950 to 59, which he thought was due not to rainfall fluctuations, but to large-scale shifting agriculture. Also in Venezuela, Lasser (1955) reported major reductions in water volume for Rio Santo Domingo as a result of shifting agriculture on steep slopes. Neither these nor other such reports that could be cited from Thailand, Pakistan, and elsewhere are based on experiments. Rather they are usually correlations that show an increasing area under shifting cultivation on one hand and a decreasing streamflow on the other. This is by no means equivalent to cause and effect. None of the workshop participants was able to provide any research evidence dealing with the effects of shifting agriculture on water yield.

The workshop group agreed that under extensive systems the effects would be minimal. Intensive systems, in which much of a watershed might be cleared and cropped at one time, should increase streamflow over the water year. Perhaps effects would be similar to those reported from Tanzania, where small landholding cultivation covering 50 percent of a 20.2-ha forest catchment over a ten-year continuous cropping period gave large increases in water yield with a doubling of the dry season base flow (Edwards and Blackie 1981).

TIMING AND DISTRIBUTION OF STREAMFLOW

Public and political conventional wisdom has frequently attributed large increases in flood frequency and intensity to shifting agriculture in the uplands (see, for example, Spears 1982). There is a dearth of good research information on which to base such statements, though for the unstable systems that result in land degradation there may well be such adverse consequences. However, much of the most serious downstream flooding and flood damage in major river systems results from precipitation characteristics and flood plain occupancy rather than from shifting agriculture.

In spite of the absence of any research results, there was agreement that extensive shifting agriculture (as delineated) would have little impact on the timing of stream discharge, unless there was a concentration of cleared land, in synchrony, on a hydrologic source area close to the stream. If this were the case, more rapid stream response might be expected.

ON-SITE EROSION

Saplaco (1981) has studied erosion from kaingin shifting agriculture in the Mt. Makiling Forest, Philippines. Soil loss from five land-use types

Table 6. Four-Year Average Soil Loss for All Slope Categories (Philippines)

Plot	Sediment Yield (t/ha)
New *kaingin*	1.672
Old *kaingin*	1.626
Plantation	0.302
Secondary forest	0.123
Grassland	0.088

Source: Saplaco (1981).
Note: Plot size was 2 × 4 m.

Table 7. Average Erosion Losses Per Day From Plots with Different Land Use (Philippines)

Plot	Sample Period (days)	Erosion Loss (gm/day)
Primary forest	197	0.20
Softwood tree fallow	197	0.29
Imperata grassland	197	0.40
New abaca plantation	197	0.41
10-year-old abaca plantation	197	0.59
New corn swidden	138[a]	3.03
	29[b]	0.65
New rice swidden	158[a]	1.45
	29[b]	0.37
2-year-old corn swidden	100[a]	12.05
	29[b]	9.81
12-year-old corn swidden	175[a]	119.31
	29[b]	6.32

Source: Adapted from Kellman (1969).
Note: Study was in Mindanao, where annual precipitation averages 422 cm with little seasonal variation. These were small plots (8 m²) located on 25-percent slope. Period under observation was January to October with the swidden treatments starting in mid-February. These results cannot be extrapolated to watersheds, and the table is presented to serve a qualitative rather than quantitative purpose.
[a]Cropping period.
[b]Intercropping period.

was measured (Table 6). New kaingin had the most severe erosion, and grassland had the least for all slope categories. The grassland was ungrazed; hence it produced the lowest sediment yield. For the southern Philippines (Mindanao), Kellman (1969) showed that crop type, length of cropping period, and vegetation cover affected erosion (Table 7).

Brunig et al. (1975) reports that shifting cultivation in Sabah, Malaysia during the cropping years gave rates of erosion of 0.5 to 2 mm (10 to 40 t/

ha) under natural forest. An erosion experiment with volcanic soil in the prehumid mountains south of Bandung, Indonesia showed little soil lost in the first year of cropping after clearing primary forest and planting dry rice in catchments of 4 to 85 ha (unterraced) and 8 to 65 ha (terraced) (Gonggrijp 1941). However, in the second year, losses of 50 t/ha from the former and half as much from the latter were recorded. In pilot studies in Nigeria, Lal (1981) reported soil erosion rates of 0.01 t/ha/yr for traditional forest clearing with seeding of maize and cassava.

Nye and Greenland (1960) in their major publication "The Soil under Shifting Agriculture," summarized their findings as follows:

> Against this general long-term background we may now consider the effects of erosion during a single period of cropping.
>
> When a forest fallow is cleared and burned nearly all the protective cover of vegetation and most of the litter are consumed, and the porous, granular mineral surface, which is mixed with finely divided partially decomposed litter and covered with a thin layer of ash, is bared to the shattering action of the heavy rain. The remains of the litter are rapidly decomposed, and the ash is washed into the soil, or with exceptionally heavy rain on a relatively impermeable soil it may be washed off the surface. Nevertheless the constitution of the soil is sufficiently stable to survive this onslaught for a few weeks until the early planted crops form a protective cover. The effects are mitigated by the fact that the plots cleared are small and are usually surrounded by undisturbed fallow so that run-off has little chance to accumulate; and by the fact that the stable surface granules of soil are little disturbed by cultivation. Gullying is rare since the shallow surface roots of the forest trees are left in the ground, and effectively counter concentrated flow. Further erosion depends on the extent to which the soil is exposed during the subsequent cropping. The common practice of planting a mixture of perennial crops is very effective in maintaining a cover. Given small clearings, slopes not exceeding 50 percent, and good crop cover, erosion on latosols under native practice is seldom serious.

The longer the cropping period compared with the fallowing, the more serious will be the erosion. In summary, however, it would seem that the erosion horrors attributed to shifting agriculture have been overemphasized, or at least overextended from areas which are under an unstable system to areas of traditional shifting agriculture. Sanchez (1979) gives expression to this in an illuminating anecdote on searching for soil erosion in the humid tropics of Latin America:

> I recently traveled extensively through the Amazon of Brazil,

Peru and Ecuador and the Colombian and Ecuadorian sierras looking at erosion problems. Two conclusions can be made from these
visual observations: (1) The extent of obvious gully erosion in shifting cultivation or pasture systems of the Amazon is insignificant.
One can see erosion caused by road construction, urban development, and drainage outlets—civil engineering erosion. (2) The extent
of soil erosion in the Andean region is high in ustic soil moisture
regimes, with a strong dry season, but also very limited in the udic,
high-rainfall upland areas. Again, most of the obvious erosion observed in the latter areas was directly caused by civil engineering and
not agronomic miscalculation.

The reason for the above generalizations is quite simple: the best
protection against erosion is to have a plant canopy to protect the soil.
In high-rainfall areas, whether on the mountains or in the Amazon
basin, there is always something growing, perhaps just weeds or secondary fallow. Nevertheless, the soil is protected, except for the cru-
cial one or two months after burning, but even then the tangle of
charred logs, tree stumps, and partially burned material provides a
degree of cover. I am more concerned about large-scale erosion in
the ustic highlands of Latin America, which appear to be more fragile ecosystems than the selvas themselves.

SEDIMENT IN STREAMS

There are few data on the effects of extensive shifting agriculture on
stream sediment. Scott (1974) carried out studies of shifting cultivation
and grassland formation in the tropical rain forest area of the Gran Pajonal of Peru, and showed that sediment yield from new swidden was
higher than from either forest or grassland. However, these were field
boundary effects and do not relate directly to the sediment load of streams
emanating from the watershed. Shifting agriculture, by its nature, results
in a mosaic pattern of field and fallow forest or grass, and therefore sediment produced by the cultivation may be trapped downslope by the fallow
land. Streams may therefore show little change in sediment load unless the
clearing is at streamside.

NUTRIENT OUTFLOW

Slash-and-burn agriculture is based on cultivated crop response to the
accumulated nutrients released from the forest vegetation following
burning. The available nutrients decline due to removal in crops harvested, oxidation of organic matter, and leaching, or to erosion and runoff
due to rainfall. When the level has reached a point where crop yields are
no longer satisfactory (and weeds and pests become too troublesome), the

plot is fallowed and a new area is cleared and burned. Thus, some of the nutrients are lost from the site, and some of these do move into the groundwater and streams. It is widely held that the fertility of the soil cannot be maintained under shifting cultivation. For example, FAO (1958) states that "at each turn of the cycle the soil becomes more depleted of nutrients and its productivity is less, and more short-lived." On low-nutrient-status soils in Venezuelan Amazonia, Jordan (1980) studied nutrient leaching following clearing and burning of tropical rain forest. There were large losses of K, M_g, and nitrates from the plot allowed to regrow immediately and the plot put into cassava (manioc) with some pineapple, cashew, and platano. The cultivated site was maintained for three years, and this plot lost more P, NH_4-N, and especially Ca, to the point where Jordan suggested that nutrient losses under such practice would hinder the eventual recovery of the forest.

Nye and Greenland (1960), in their major work on "The Soil under Shifting Cultivation," examine the world literature and come up with an equivocal answer, depending on soils, vegetation, crops, and length of fallow. In some areas of the world, this practice has been going on for hundreds of years, without apparent decline in productivity over the cycles.

SUMMARY AND IMPLICATIONS

Shifting agricultural practices, whether extensive or intensive, do have impacts on the hydrologic, erosional, and nutrient characteristics of watersheds. There is no gainsaying that dense populations of nontraditional cultivators cropping in steep terrain in the tropics and subtropics and continually advancing into steeper upper watersheds and more marginal environments are having significant and deleterious effects on the nutrient outflow, peak stormflows, erosion, and stream sedimentation. Migrant groups or new colonists with little understanding of the ecosystem's carrying capacity have produced off-site effects that have alarmed observers and downstream populations. They have given shifting agriculture in general an image that has led foresters and land-use planners to regard this farming system as the principal villain in the watershed drama. There are few reliable data to support this belief, but one can piece together evidence from watershed research dealing with some agriculture or effects of fire. For instance, in unstable systems in the tropical dry forests, slash-and-burn agriculture by nontraditional farmers may employ intensive burning over large areas. One may then with some justification take note of results from Australia or Arizona, where wildfire in gauged watersheds produced dramatic increases in stormflows and stream sediment (Glendenning et al. 1961; Brown 1972). Specific research is needed for tropical moist and tropical dry forests in gauged watersheds on this important land-use topic.

A similar lack of data plagues the situation with extensive, sustainable shifting agriculture. Observation, intuition, and analysis of the hydrologic processes involved indicates that the effects on the variables considered in this workshop are localized and transitory. Erosion is an inevitable consequence of the process of clearing, burning, and cultivating on sloping land. The variations—in degree of slope, in period of cropping, in crop type, in length of cleared slope, in tools used, and in whether the slash is burned or merely chopped and scattered—all make generalizations about quantification meaningless. Suffice it to say that in the sustainable systems as delineated in this section, soil losses from the area are not a cause of productivity decline and hence abandonment of the area, except over very long peiods of time. While nutrients are lost from the cleared plot, they are replaced in the fallow period. Some of these systems have been in place for many generations without serious land degradation or nutrient impoverishment.

Moreover, because of the mosaic pattern of surrounding fallowed land, what erosion does take place is usually trapped at the plot boundary. Thus stream sediment increases are not an inevitable consequence of stable shifting agriculture (unless the clearing is on sloping land adjacent to a water channel). And because the area cultivated in a watershed in stable systems at any one time is usually less than 20 percent of the entire area, the effects on stormflow peaks is probably fairly small. Total water yield from a watershed subject to stable shifting agriculture is thought to be greater than from an undisturbed watershed.

On the basis of evidence available to the workshop participants, there seems no compelling reason to move *traditional* shifting agriculturists out of watershed areas in the name of improved soil and water regimes if they are engaged in sustainable, stable systems. This would not be true for watersheds providing untreated water for municipal domestic use. In other watersheds, however, it might be much more effective to work with shifting agriculturists to help them in maintaining stable systems. This might take the form of assistance in obtaining suitable food and forest trees for planting in an agroforestry system. The program of Forest Occupancy Management, which is being attempted in the Philippines (Duldulao 1981), is a positive overture in this direction.

Unstable slash-and-burn, carried out by migrants who maintain cash cropping until the site is impoverished or converted to a degraded grassland, is quite a different matter, and the implications of this are discussed in other chapters.

3
Harvesting Fuelwood and Lopping Fodder

The forest continues to be the major source of energy for cooking and warmth in many tropical countries. Lopping twigs and branches to provide foliage as fodder for livestock is also a widespread practice in developing countries. In some countries, the practices are often associated. As defined herein, the impacts of these activities will be based on sustainable levels of harvesting (not overcutting or overlopping the renewable growth) and on situations where there is no roading and no use of machinery in the harvest or extraction.

Where the level of fuelwood harvesting is so great that the forest is being eliminated, it is considered a conversion to another use. Such levels of cutting in the tropics are often associated with grazing practices, and in reality the forest is being grazed (see Chapter 5 for impacts) or is being gradually converted to grassland/savanna (see Chapter 8 for impacts). The same is true for excessive fodder lopping. In cases where overharvesting results in death of the trees (and then usually their removal as fuel), the forest is actually undergoing conversion. Usually this is a conversion to grazing, and again, effects are presented under "Grazing on Forestland" (Chapter 5) or "Conversion to Grassland/Savanna" (Chapter 8). These unsustainable levels of harvesting unfortunately are all too common in the uplands of the tropical world and too often result in degraded lands, which aggravate the rural poverty situation and which produce harmful off-site effects downstream. The impact of these activities tends to decrease with distance from a village or settlement, and there is probably a gradient from nonsustainable to sustainable cutting and lopping as the distance from the settlement increases.

Where roads and machinery are used to harvest fuelwood, the effects of such action are dealt with in the chapter on "Harvesting Commercial Wood."

The major hydrologic impact of sustainable fuelwood cutting or fodder lopping occurs because of a reduction in the canopy. This results in decreased interception, increased throughfall and decreased evapotranspiration.

GROUNDWATER, SPRINGS, AND WELLS

No evidence was available to indicate the impact of sustainable fuelwood cutting and fodder lopping on groundwater, springs, and wells. In theory, the increased throughfall and reduced evapotranspiration might increase the amount of groundwater recharge, and levels might rise.

STREAMFLOW QUANTITY

Since sustainable fuelwood harvesting or fodder lopping is similar to forest thinning, results from forest thinning activities were deemed applicable. Temperate zone research indicates first year increases in streamflow in proportion to the degree of canopy removal (Douglass and Swank 1975). This effect was confirmed by a study in the Philippines involving different degrees of thinning of Benguet pine (Veracion and Lopez 1975). Annual cutting or lopping on a sustainable basis should result in somewhat increased annual water yield.

TIMING AND DISTRIBUTION OF STREAMFLOW

There are no good data coming directly from research on how fuelwood cutting affects the timing of streamflow. On some of the outer islands of Fiji, where villagers were using up to 1,300 kg per capita per year in a seasonal climate, the local wisdom is that low flows in streams have been further reduced by this activity. This does not coincide with results from thinning experiments in controlled catchments in the temperate zone, where cutting of trees (reducing canopy) changes distribution by increasing flow levels in those months when flows were lowest (Douglass 1981).

This topic is of considerable interest in Fiji, where there is some controversy over the effects on low flows of streams of the establishment and subsequent thinning and harvesting of pines in the Fiji Pine Corporation scheme. A study has been initiated in Fiji, partly as an outgrowth of this workshop.

ON-SITE EROSION

Since by definition of this activity, no roads or machinery are involved in the harvest, the main causes of erosion are not operative. Manual or animal power removal of cut material may result in some dragging of material, which could initiate some channeling of water and then erosion. The intensity of the activity, the slope, and the nature of the soil are key factors. In Taiwan, Yuan lin Lin (1981, Pers. Comm.) reported on a study in which 550,000 m^3/yr of fuelwood were removed from a 2,100-ha watershed with a resulting soil loss of 2 mm per year. This was regarded as normal and tolerable for the particular conditions of topography, soils, and climate.

Sustainable fuelwood cutting itself should have no effect on rate of erosion. Even if the levels of cutting are sustainable, however, the way in which the cut material is removed could increase the erosion rate or initiate gullies. If minimizing erosion is the concern, then efforts should focus on extraction methods. Repeatedly dragging material downhill on the same track, even by hand or with animal power, is likely to result in gullying.

Fodder lopping has little effect on erosion unless it be erosion on the trails used in harvesting. Unfortunately, this practice is often combined with livestock grazing in the steep lands of the Himalayan arc, and Megahan (1981, Pers. Comm.) and others report that there the pressures to overharvest in "the commons" result in the death of trees, overgrazing, increased runoff, and gully erosion.

SEDIMENT IN STREAMS

Since sustainable harvesting of fuelwood and fodder as defined is without roading and machinery, it does not significantly increase on-site erosion. There would therefore be no increase in sediment delivery to the streams.

NUTRIENT OUTFLOW

Although nutrients in the form of wood and leaves are removed from the system, and such a drain increases with decreasing rotation in the case of fast-growing trees, the decreasing rotation and the increase in nutrients washed out of the forest and into streams are not deemed to be of great importance under the conditions specified.

SUMMARY AND IMPLICATIONS

Policies with respect to use of fuelwood and fodder foliage in important watershed areas should concentrate on two factors:

1. Restricting the intensity of harvesting to long-term sustainable levels so that the forest remains a forest and is not on a slow or rapid conversion curve to another use with less desirable soil and water impacts.
2. Controlling the way in which material is removed from the forest. Use of roading and machinery requires special measures to minimize adverse changes in runoff, erosion, and sedimentation. (See Megahan 1977, "Reducing erosional impact of roads"; Gilmour 1977, "Logging and the environment, with particular reference to soil and stream

protection in tropical rainforest situations.") Even manual removal or use of animal power may need to be controlled or guided so that the impacts are diffused over the area rather than concentrated, and minimized rather than maximized through judicious allocation of cutting or fodder lopping blocks.

With control, there is no intrinsic reason why harvesting fuelwood and lopping fodder need be prohibited in watersheds. Statements such as Openshaw's (1974) that the principal cause of the recent floods in the Indian subcontinent was the removal of the tree cover in the catchment areas for firewood (and shifting cultivation) are apt to lead to overreaction. This assertion is fuzzy at best and inaccurate at worst. *How* the fuelwood is removed, and whether the forest remains forest or is transformed into inappropriately used grazing land or cropland, has much more to do with the downstream ills often ascribed to fuelwood cutting. Much of the steep Himalayan foothill land has indeed been degraded through uncontrolled fuelwood cutting and fodder lopping, and has become overgrazed denuded land — not forest. This *conversion* has indeed caused increased runoff, increased erosion, and increased sediment loads in streams and rivers. Flooding has been aggravated, but this is not equivalent to statements that fuelwood cutting is the principal cause of major lower basin floods.

4
Harvesting Commercial Wood

A large area of tropical forest has been subjected to commercial wood harvesting since the end of World War II, and the area logged increases almost every year. Between 1950 and 1973, the developed world's imports of tropical hardwoods increased from 5.2 million m³ to 52 million m³ (Grainger 1980). Domestic use of the hardwoods by tropical countries also increased dramatically in that period, adding to the impact. FAO (1979) estimates that more than 1 billion m³, one third of the wood removed from the world's forests for human use, comes from the tropics. Currently, more than 70 percent of tropical wood exported is from Asia and the Pacific (FAO 1979). Wood exports from the tropics have been increasing at a rate of 7.1 percent in volume annually over the years 1970 to 1980 (U.S. Interagency Task Force on Tropical Forests 1980).

The impact of commercial wood harvesting on the watershed variables considered here depends on several factors, including:

- The amount of canopy removed;
- The amount of biomass removed (including how much slash remains on the area);
- The product removal methods;
- The timing with respect to wet and dry season;
- The soil, geologic conditions, and topography;
- The extent, nature, and usage of roads, skid trails, and landings;
- The methods of slash disposal and site preparation;
- The promptness with which regeneration occurs (or reforestation is carried out);
- The presence or absence of adequate riparian buffer strips; and
- The nature of climatic events following disturbance.

When considering commercial harvesting of trees, it is necessary to make a distinction between the effects of reducing the amount of forest cover and the effects of removing the exploited products (logging). Moreover, it is helpful to distinguish, within the logging activity, between commonly used practices that give scant regard to impacts on soil and water, and those "improved" harvesting methods that include a major component of environmental protection with regard to watershed values. This chapter will therefore attempt to identify research results by whether they are:

- Impacts of canopy reduction or removal (herein called "cutting");
- Impacts of commonly used logging methods; or
- Impacts of improved watershed protection logging.

Figure 2 illustrates some likely changes in the hydrologic behavior of a watershed following partial or complete canopy removal by tree cutting. The variables considered in this book are in the lower tiers of the diagram. The mechanisms or processes directly affected by tree removal are in the top tier, boxes A through E, and the linkages are indicated by arrows and intermediate boxes. The word "likely" is used because the reaction of a watershed to such a change is the result of a complex interaction of a range of variables, not the least of which is the amount of canopy or tree removal, from slight (as under selection cutting) to complete (as in clearfelling).

In general, the initial, direct impacts of harvesting (called deforestation in Figure 2), are as follows (Megahan 1982, Pers. Comm.):

1. Reduces protection—including tree canopy, understory canopy and litter. This results in greater raindrop impact energy (usually) and bares soil.
2. Changes soil properties—including compaction, disaggregation, loss of organic matter, water repellancy, etc. This results in reduced infiltration and increased soil erodibility.
3. Reduces transpiration, increases air movement, and changes temperature. This changes evapotranspiration, usually reducing it.
4. Reduces root mass. This reduces soil shear strength, which will not be as serious in coppicing tree species.
5. Loses water capture function in a "cloud forest" situation. This reduces effective on-site precipitation.

GROUNDWATER, SPRINGS, AND WELLS

Reduction in canopy from tree felling results in reduced evapotranspiration until the canopy is restored by regeneration. This reduction should result in higher stored soil moisture and thus make more water available to recharge groundwater, springs, and wells. Throughfall is usually increased because of the reduction in interception, thus allowing a greater percentage of the rainfall to reach the forest floor (particularly important

29

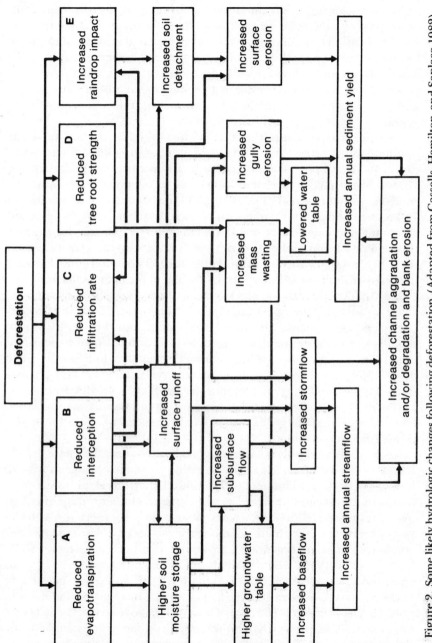

Figure 2. Some likely hydrologic changes following deforestation. (Adapted from Cassells, Hamilton, and Saplaco 1982)

during light intensity, short duration precipitation events and of minor consequence during high intensity and prolonged storms). Any additional precipitation reaching the forest floor will either infiltrate the soil, contribute to surface runoff, or evaporate. Increased raindrop impact will be minimal if it is possible to retain forest root mat and litter, and in such a case, reduced infiltration rates should not occur. Thus, water movement processes in forests should result in a net increase in groundwater following canopy reduction, with the effect persisting until full canopy is restored.

A special situation exists where "cloud forests" (also variously known as montane dwarf forests and elfin woodlands) or coastal fog forests exist, capturing occult precipitation and adding it to the water budget of the system. Ekern (1964) in Hawaii found that plantations of *Araucaria heterophylla*, with an annual rainfall of 2,600 mm, condensed an additional 760 mm from cloud formations. In Mexico, Vogelmann (1973) obtained substantial increases in dry season precipitation by inducing fog capture through simulation of the effect of trees (102 percent increase at one station). In coastal "fog forests" in Oregon, Isaac (1946) found annual precipitation of 252 cm in the forest, versus 200 cm in the open. Removal of the canopy reduces this capture and may result in decreased groundwater recharge. Zadroga (1981) pointed out that: "The typical positive effect occurs when cloud banks enshroud mountain slopes during dry season months when little or no rainfall (vertical) is recorded. Under these conditions moisture may condense upon exposed vegetational surfaces and drip or run down stems to the ground, thereby recharging soil and groundwater supplies and thus maintaining stream discharge." However, no experimental results are yet available to support or quantify the presumed effect of a decrease in groundwater from a removal of cloud forest (Zadroga 1981, Pers. Comm.).

Aside from cloud forests, increasing heights of water tables have usually followed cutting of forests in areas where permanent water tables are found (Wicht 1949). Gilmour (1977b) showed in a tropical rainforest situation an approximate 10-percent increase in groundwater storage after logging. O'Loughlin (1981, Pers. Comm.) suggested that experience with forest cutting on flat valley bottom lands in the wet parts of New Zealand is for an increase in groundwater level. However, he calls attention to one study by McDonald (1955), who was unable to detect differences between forested and adjacent cleared sites. Boughton's (1970) review of experience in Australia and elsewhere showed almost total consensus on increases in groundwater following clearing. The Working Group on Influence of Man on the Hydrologic Cycle (1972) reported the only example of the reverse effect from a situation in Russia where most precipitation occurred as snow on frozen soils.

In the case of forest harvesting, and not forest clearing for other use, any increase should be temporary and will diminish as the new forest regrows. Roads are a confounding element, however, since they may cut across groundwater aquifers, especially springs, and channel the water off-site. Careful road layout in improved watershed protection logging generally can avoid this problem. Soil compaction by heavy machinery in highly mechanized logging can reduce infiltration and hence decrease groundwater accessions, but reduced groundwater levels have not been found in any documented research.

STREAMFLOW QUANTITY

Almost every well-designed experiment has shown increased water yield as a response to forest cutting, and in general the increase is proportional to the amount of canopy removed. The increase declines as full forest returns to the site. The most recent review of catchment experiments has been undertaken by Bosch and Hewlett (1982). In assessing the results from 94 catchments, they have added the results of 55 experiments to those assessed by Hibbert (1967) and come up with the same conclusion: no experiments in deliberately reducing vegetative cover (e.g., by logging) caused reductions in yield. Moreover, they even suggest some predictive generalizations as follows:*

- Coniferous and eucalypt cover types have approximately a 40 mm increase in water yield per 10 percent reduction in cover.
- Deciduous hardwoods have approximately a 25 mm increase in yield per 10 percent reduction in cover.

The paired catchment results from Bosch and Hewlett (1982) are shown in Figure 3 for different percentages of cover reduction (including scrub). There are few paired-catchment studies in the humid tropics, where so much logging and forest conversion are now occurring. Figure 4 shows the results from one of the classic studies—Watershed 17 at Coweeta (U.S.), which was clearcut and then cut annually for seven years to keep regrowth in check. Bosch and Hewlett suggested that the increases due to cutting are greatest in high rainfall areas but that the effect is shorter due to more rapid regrowth.

In Taiwan, Lin (1981, Pers. Comm.) reported paired-catchment results showing similar kinds of increases following clearcutting and skyline logging, with first-year streamflow exceeding the expected value by 292 mm

*It should be kept in mind that these are rough generalizations and may be wide of the mark for any particular environment and treatment.

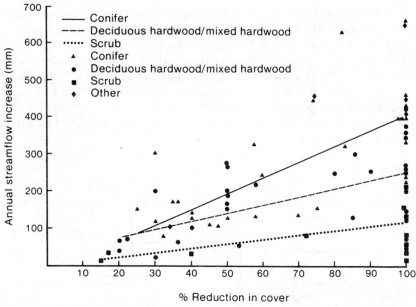

Figure 3. Yield increases following changes in vegetation cover. (Adapted from Bosch and Hewlett 1982)

(48 percent), with greatest increases (108 percent) occurring in the dry season. A clearcut experimental watershed in central Taiwan is shown in Figure 5.

A major exception seems to be where occult precipitation is a major factor in the water budget. In coastal Oregon, Harr (1980) found no increase in water yield following patch clearcutting. He attributed this to the loss of the fog drip accessions to precipitation.

On some watershed experiments in Japan under winter snow patterns, Nakano (1967) found only minor increases in annual flow in some small mountain drainages, though on others, increases of from 8 to 24 percent were obtained. However, in subsequent analysis and modeling for five catchments, Nakano (1971) reported increases of 10, 30, 33, 43, and 46 percent. In tropical humid Queensland also, no dramatic increases in yield were observed following logging (Gilmour et al. 1982). While statistically significant increases in monthly totals were obtained following clearing for pasture (a 10 percent annual increase or 293 mm), no significant increase occurred from "unconstrained" logging. Gilmour et al. attribute the anomaly of their results to the relatively minor role of vegetation changes in the situation of soils with limited water storage capacity (20 cm), overland flow even under undisturbed forest, and an intense monsoon storm pattern (e.g., maximum 6-min storm rainfall equivalent to 70 to 150 mm/

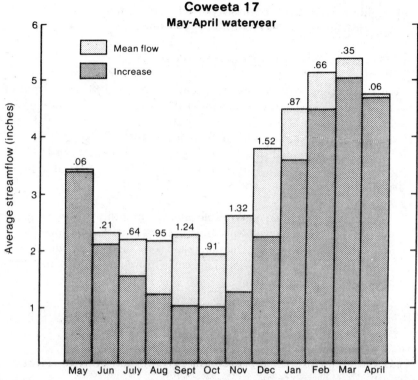

Figure 4. Average monthly streamflow and increase in flow during seven years of annual recutting on Watershed 17. (Douglass and Swank 1972)

hr). Logging did, however, have a marked effect on erosion and sediment and caused small increases in peak discharge.

Total annual water yield increases have not been shown to change according to whether the logging was done with or without watershed conservation methods. However, one of the consequences of the lower amount of site disturbance that accompanies conservation logging methods would be the more rapid recovery to the prelogging regime, with more rapid and complete regeneration.

Partial cuts result in smaller increases in yield, but the shorter cutting cycle for a watershed, which could result from partial cutting, would mean more frequent occurrences of increased yields. Results from catchment studies in New Zealand give some specifics on this aspect of water yield. In a 2,600-mm rainfall regime at Maimai, 100 percent clearfelling (slash burned) gave a 650-mm increased annual yield, and 75 percent clearfelling (slash burned) gave a 540-mm increase (Pearce 1980, Pearce et al. 1980). On a nearby catchment with annual precipitation of 1,550 mm,

O'Loughlin (1981, Pers. Comm.) reported a 200-mm increase from a 50-percent clearfelling.

TIMING AND DISTRIBUTION OF STREAMFLOW

With the exception of the results obtained by Harr (1980), who found a decrease in low-flow months following patch clearcutting of a forest where some of the fog occult precipitation capture was lost, other studies where changes occurred showed increases in low-season flows. The Coweeta (U.S.) clearcut watershed (not logged—simply cut) showed this low-flow augmentation clearly (see Figure 3). Of this temperate-zone, deciduous, hardwood forest, Douglass and Swank (1975) stated:

> A forest cover had no measurable effect on monthly flow when soil storage space was charged with moisture (season of high flows). Before and after clearcutting, the watershed contained nearly equal volumes of water during late winter and early spring, and the hydrologic response was about the same.

Figure 5. Taiwan Forest Research Institute 5.8-ha clearcut watershed (average 40-percent slope, 2,500 mm rain) to determine effect on water yield and distribution.

As the growing season progressed, however, the difference in moisture storage between the cut and forested conditions progressively increased. Drainage reaching the stream shortly after a rain was proportional to the moisture storage difference between the forest and clearcut conditions. Streamflow increases began in about June and increased in magnitude as the growing season advanced. In September, October, and November, streamflow was increased by 100 percent. This is precisely the season when demand for water is greatest and unregulated flow is lowest. Large increases continued until December and then declined as the difference in moisture storage between clearcut and forested conditions declined. For treatments which produce less drastic storage differences, recharge occurs more quickly and increases are not delayed as late into the winter.

Stormflows were increased less than 20 percent in the first years after cutting at Coweeta, and the regrowing forest reduced stormflows below pretreatment levels after about eight years (Douglass, 1981, Pers. Comm.). It should be kept in mind that these watershed forests were cut but the products were not removed by logging.

Work at Hubbard Brook (U.S.), also with no logging, confirms the general effects set forth. Even with logging, Nakano (1971) in Japan found similar results, with little or no increase during the wet season (snow), and the greatest increases occurred in the dry season (growing season). In New Zealand, however, where logging was carried out, Pearce et al. (1980) reported that in an evergreen podocarp-beech-mixed-hardwood forest catchment that was 75 percent clearcut, increases occurred in all months of the year. Sixty percent of the increased yield appeared in larger stormflow volumes. However, the time to peak discharge from the initial rise of individual storm hydrographs was not influenced significantly by the harvesting. More recently, both partial and clearfelling treatments on four other watersheds at the same experimental site in northern South Island gave increased yields rather uniformly across all months of the year (O'Loughlin 1981, Pers. Comm.).

In the Appalachian mountains of West Virginia (U.S.), a watershed clearcut and logged gave significantly increased yields during the growing season months (including the usual low-flow months), extending from June through November, with only slightly increased yield during the dormant season (Reinhart et al. 1963). Diameter limit and selection logging increases were more apparent in the driest months (September, October). The cutting had a strong effect on low flows, and the heavier the cut, the greater the effect. In the two years following the harvesting, the days of low streamflow were reduced from 145 to 43 on the clearcut, from 103 to 29 on the diameter limit, from 75 to 40 on the extensive selection, and from 85 to

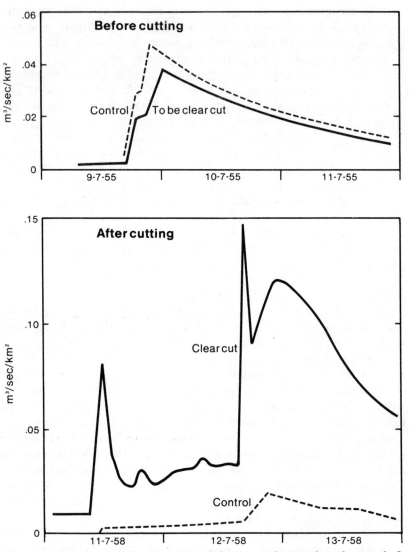

Figure 6. Sample storm hydrographs of clearcut and control catchments before and after treatment in West Virginia, U.S.A. (Reinhart et al. 1963)

67 on the intensive selection (Reinhart et al., 1963). As to effects on high flow, storm flow from the clearcut watershed was several times that from the control. Figure 6 shows sample storm hydrographs on three successive days in the growing season for the clearcut and the control. The authors summarized the effect of cutting on flood flows as follows: The effect of heavy cutting on high flows was variable, depending on the presence or

absence of snow, antecedent soil moisture, and probably other factors; in the dormant season the effect was not usually great; in the region of the experiments, flood occurrence was greater in the dormant season.

One of the few studies from the tropics was carried out in North Queensland, Australia. Gilmour (1977b) stated that prior to logging, North Creek ceased to flow some years for varying periods before the beginning of the wet season, but that after treatment the creek remained perennial. The highest percentage increases were in low-flow periods.

The Coweeta results of studying the impact of timber harvest on timing and distribution of yield are the most detailed and long term. Douglass (1981, Pers. Comm.) summarized these so well in his presentation at the workshop that the full text appears as Appendix B. Included therein is a brief physical description of the Coweeta area that may aid in judging differences and similarities with tropical conditions. The Coweeta studies showed greater increases in stormflow volume, peak flow, and stormflow duration with cutting, and these increases were greater in the watersheds with deeper soils at lower elevation (e.g., 40-mm stormflow increase versus 25-mm increase for shallower soils, higher elevation). Carefully constructed roads and good harvesting techniques produced larger increases in these hydrograph parameters than cutting the forest without harvesting, indicating the important effect of skid trails and roads (Douglass 1981, Pers. Comm.). There is an implication that poorly constructed roads would increase stormflow parameters even more.

ON-SITE EROSION

Erosion is not usually an important process in the undisturbed forest, but it can occur. Where mineral soil is exposed in a forest, soil detachment due to splash erosion can exceed that occurring in the open, primarily due to larger drop size. This was the conclusion of a study of kinetic energy of raindrops and surface erosion in New Zealand. Mosley (in press) showed that the kinetic energy of throughfall under beech-podocarp-hardwood-forest canopy was always greater than that of rainfall in the open, notwithstanding interception losses. During a typical rain event in which 51 mm fell in 36 hours, the total kinetic energy of throughfall was 1.5 times greater, and the mean amount of sand splashed from cups was 3.1 times greater under the canopy than in the open. Soemarwoto (1982, Pers. Comm.) also found greater splash erosion under tree canopies in Indonesia, with larger drops occurring from leaf drip than in open rainfall.

While overland flow with surface erosion potential is not considered an important problem in most temperate watersheds (Hewlett and Hibbert 1967), widespread overland flow occurred in an undisturbed Queensland, Australia, rainforest catchment during the monsoon and postmonsoon seasons (Gilmour et al. 1982). This was attributed to low permeability of the soil below 20 cm and to the precipitation pattern. Sheet erosion occurred under these conditions. That it was not more serious, the authors explained as follows:

> However, it is equally apparent from the monitoring studies that the vegetation and condition of the soil surface are major influences on the catchment's erosion generation response during wet season storms. The undisturbed rainforest with its different vegetation layers, dense undergrowth of saplings, lawyer palms, vines, ferns and patches of decaying organic litter, provides some initial protection against raindrop impact. The extensive network of tree trunks, small stems, buttressed roots and surface roots also provides many impediments to downslope sediment transport that would otherwise occur given the presence of widespread overland flow. In addition, the surface soil has been ameliorated by the continual incorporation of organic matter to provide a thin but very stable and highly permeable zone.

Disturbance by logging under such conditions obviously has the potential for serious increases in erosion. Cassells (1981, Pers. Comm.) suggested that while overland flow might be a rare event in some humid temperate watersheds, the experience in Queensland, (and perhaps that in other monsoonal climates such as Taiwan, Fiji, and the Philippines—all represented at the workshop) indicated substantial overland flow and consequently some erosion, and certainly high erosion hazard. Peh (1980) also suggested that overland flow is a significant erosional and hydrological process under tropical rainforest conditions in Malaysia.

When commercial wood harvesting occurs, erosion increases markedly. That this is due mainly to the soil disturbance occasioned by extraction of the cut material is illustrated in the Coweeta (U.S.) experimental watersheds. Douglass (1981, Pers. Comm.) reported that there was still no overland flow with clearcutting (but no product removal) and hence no increase in erosion. He stated that on these relatively deep soils where infiltration exceeded maximum rainfall by threefold to twentyfold even after cutting, erosion from the land surface does not occur if timber is cut but products are not removed nor roads built. This conclusion is supported by the clearcut-but-no-product-removal experience at Hubbard Brook (U.S.) (Likens et al. 1970).

However, studies of mass erosion on unstable slopes give one pause to wonder even about tree cutting with no logging in these special "critical" areas. Mass erosion is attributed to increases in the saturated soil zone and decreased root shear strength caused by root decay following cutting. Where logging is involved, the situation may be exacerbated by oversteepened slopes in road cuttings, often continually wet at the toe of the slope. Accelerated landslide activity following timber harvest has been reported in the western United States, Taiwan, Japan, and particularly in New Zealand.

In New Zealand, studies on the influence of timber removal on slope stability and mass erosion show variation from one site to another depending on geology, slope steepness and length, and rainfall. In Mawhera State Forest, clearfelling increased landslide densities from 1 per km² to 20 per km² (O'Loughlin and Pearce 1976). The importance of tree roots for soil shear resistance has been emphasized (O'Loughlin 1974; O'Loughlin and Watson 1979). Under conditions of soil saturation, 80 percent of the total shear strength may be attributed to tree roots. Under New Zealand's conditions, tree roots lose their tensile root strength very quickly after the death of a tree.

In the Maimai (N.Z.) experimental watersheds, 98 percent of the slope failures occurred during two exceptional storms, which occupied only 0.15 percent of the total study time (6 years) (O'Loughlin et al. in press). In one storm with a return period of about 10 years, no landslides were recorded in undisturbed watersheds or those that had been clearfelled for less than 20 months. However, the storm caused 18 landslides on the slopes of four watersheds which had been clearfelled for 20 months or more. The volume of landslide debris moved from slopes to streambeds in these watersheds averaged 0.44 m³/ha. The loss of tree root stabilization appears to have been a dominant factor in landslide initiation.

These studies indicate the site-specific nature of the effects of timber harvesting. In many areas slope stability and mass erosion are not of great importance (e.g., at Coweeta, U.S.). Areas with slope stability problems can be identified in advance.

The way in which products are removed, involving log landings, skid trails, and roads, certainly produces the most serious adverse watershed consequences in commercial wood harvesting, both in tropic and temperate zones. In reporting on the impact of commercial harvesting in the hill *Dipterocarpus* forests of Peninsular Malaysia, Burgess (1973) found that approximately 16 percent of the area was disturbed in road surfaces, road spoil, and log landings, and that these areas showed severe erosion, especially gullying. In Queensland, Australia, the area disturbed by logging is commonly up to 25 percent of the total. In the Northwestern United States, the variation in bare area following logging, depending on the method, was shown by Rice et al. (1972). For jammer logging group selection, 25 to 30 percent bare; for high lead clearcut, 6.2 percent; for skyline clearcut, 2.0 percent; and for helicopter clearcut, 1.2 percent.

All workshop participants confirmed the accelerated erosion from these disturbed areas. Experimental evidence was produced from Australia, Japan, and New Zealand (for example: Gilmour [1977a], Tsukamoto [1975],

TABLE 8. The Influence of the Regrowth that Occurs in Erosion Rates on Skidding Roads in an Indonesian Logging Situation[a]

Plots/Treatments	Erosion t/ha/mo	Runoff m³/ha/mo
Newly constructed and used skid road	12.90	189.14
Newly constructed but unused skid road	10.80	148.56
Two years abandoned skid road	6.15	42.70
Three years abandoned skid road	3.20	19.22
Forest undisturbed no skid road	0.00	2.09

Source: Adapted from Rusland and Manan (1980).
[a]Slope 8–10 percent; precipitation, 2,429 mm/yr; Latosol; plot size, 4m × 2m; observation period, 5 months.

and O'Loughlin and Pearce [1976]). A study of erosion differences between undisturbed forest and skidding roads in a tropical country (Indonesia) is shown in Table 8 (Rusland and Manan 1980). The influence of the regrowth that occurs in the skid trails after abandonment is evident. Lim Suan (1980) in the Philippines reported that of the different disturbed areas in a logged-over site, the most severe soil erosion occurred in plots on the road fillslopes.

The importance of roads has been emphasized in United States studies of erosion following timber harvest. In steep central Idaho, Megahan and Kidd (1972) found over a six-year study period that surface erosion per unit of area disturbed by roads averaged 220 times greater than that on nearby undisturbed lands; erosion on the area disturbed only by cutting and skidding (skyline system) was only 1.6 times greater than in the undisturbed area. Megahan (1976) pointed out that in addition to reduced infiltration rates on road surfaces due to soil compaction, roads have additional features that tend to accelerate erosion: increased slope gradients on cut-and-fill slopes; interception of subsurface water flow zones; and concentration of overland flow of water on the road prism and in channels. Problems associated with roads can be reduced by proper road location and design. The 170 t/ha/yr of soil eroded from the surface of a well-designed but unsurfaced road compared with rates of 1,200 t/ha/yr for a poorly-designed one (steep grade without adequate outsloping or breaks in grade) at Coweeta (U.S.) (Hoover 1945). Gilmour et al. (1982) pointed out how important the preplanning of the road and skid trail network is for the high-erosion-potential sites in steep lands of the humid tropics where conventional ground logging can disturb up to 25 percent of the area. The FAO Conservation Guide entitled "Guidelines for Watershed Management" contains articles by Gilmour (1977a), Megahan (1977), and Rice (1977) presenting practical guidelines to reduce erosional impacts of commercial harvesting of forests.

SEDIMENT IN STREAMS

In monitored catchment research, one of the more common ways to determine the impact of harvesting commercial forest on erosion is to measure the sediment content of water flowing from the experimental area. Although this provides a general idea of treatment effects on erosion, the source of the sediment may not be known specifically. Surface erosion, mass erosion, and stream channel erosion result in sediment in streams. Eroded soil resulting from disturbance in one place on a watershed may be trapped downslope by an undisturbed area and never appear as stream sediment. The very great importance of filter/buffer strips retained in natural vegetation along watercourses is emphasized, because of this soil- (and nutrient-) trapping effect. Sediment in streams can increase not because the treatment changed the erosion rate, but because it changed the flow rate and volume in the stream so that more stream channel erosion occurs. This effect was indicated in Figure 2.

Moreover, the sediment showing up in a stream after one event, such as a storm, may have come from a temporary storage where eroded soil was deposited following its initial erosion during a previous event. A graphic display of these erosion and sediment processes was given by Megahan (1981) and is presented here as Figure 7.

For all of these reasons, there is not necessarily a direct cause-and-effect relationship between changes in on-site erosion and resulting downstream sedimentation following timber harvesting activities. Moreover, a variety of erosion processes may be acting at various locations in a basin. In addition to being dependent on the nature and severity of erosion, stream sediment is related directly to rainfall and basin relief and inversely to watershed area. However, there are several good studies that have shown increased sediment yield due to logging, and some give information about the relative effects of different kinds of logging. Most of these again are from temperate watersheds, but the processes should not differ greatly in tropical watersheds.

Logging of a tropical catchment in North Queensland, Australia, produced a two- to threefold increase in suspended sediment load at high flows. Sediment load increased from about 180 ppm before logging to about 320 ppm during the first year after logging and to about 520 ppm during the second year after logging (Gilmour 1977b). The differences between the two years were attributed to differing rainfall characteristics. At another North Queensland site involving heavy logging of virgin tropical rainforest, during high intensity rains peak concentrations at sampling stations below the logging area increased six- to twelvefold (Gilmour 1971). The sediment derived from streams flowing through undisturbed forest was largely organic, in contrast with the dominantly mineral sedi-

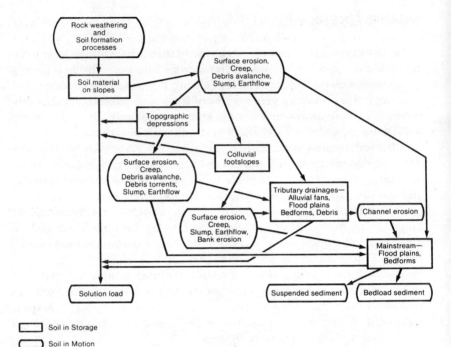

Figure 7. Erosion processes and storage locations in a watershed. (Megahan 1981)

ment in streams coming from the logged area. Gilmour reported that the principal sources of sediment were from poorly located, undrained roads and skid trails, from log landings, and from earth- and log-filled stream crossings. Sediment associated with a log landing in this study is shown in Table 9. It was evident that sediment cleared rapidly once the rain ceased, but Gilmour pointed out that these results were from a light shower and that the situation would be considerably aggravated under monsoonal con-

Table 9. Stream Sediment associated with a Log Landing Adjacent to a Stream after 8 mm of Rain between 1320 and 1340 Hours

Location	Time (hr)	Sediment Concentration (ppm)
Upstream of landing	13.45	48
Immediately downstream of landing	13.45	2,602
50 m downstream	13.50	203
400 m downstream	14.00	186
400 m downstream	15.45	21

Source: Adapted from Gilmour (1971).

ditions. He also indicated that as a result of this study, conditions were added to the timber sale agreements to minimize the effects of these sediment-producing areas, and that they were effective in reducing sediment levels. These conditions were enunciated as guidelines in the FAO "Guidelines for Watershed Management" (Gilmour 1977a).

Subsequent work in Queensland in the humid tropics, especially where substantial overland flow occurs due to low permeability of soils, has emphasized the potential for serious erosion and consequent sediment increases during and following logging (Gilmour et al. 1982). They particularly pointed out the importance of undisturbed streamside buffer strips to minimize sediment increases—both by trapping upslope erosion and by protecting the streambanks.

For Indonesia, Kuswata (1981) reported that no convincing studies have been carried out to show the effects of logging on stream sediment loads, but he stated that sediment loads of rivers within deforested areas were extremely large and a cause of national concern. Hamzah (1978) has made some observations on the effects of mechanical logging in East Kalimantan and reported increasing silt content in the river the closer the measurements were made to the logging area.

Figure 8. Experimental catchments of the New Zealand Forest Service showing clearfelling treatments and maintained riparian buffer strips. (Courtesy N.Z. Forest Research Institute)

In New Zealand, near Nelson, Graynoth (1979) reported a mean suspended yearly sediment concentration of 213 mg/l in a catchment that was clearfelled to the stream edge and roaded, as compared with a mean of 8 mg/l for an adjacent undisturbed control catchment (see Figure 8). The influence of the way in which the felled tree products are removed is also shown in another New Zealand study. O'Loughlin et al. (1980) reported sediment yields from three catchments: one control, one clearfelled and logged with a down hill cable system (no roading), and one clearfelled and logged using a skidder and roads. The annual sediment yield rates were, respectively, 33, 47, and 264 m³/km²/yr. A subsequent and as yet unpublished study of the effects of clearfelling and skidder logging in beech-podocarp-hardwood forest showed an increase from approximately 5 m³/km²/yr to 16 m³/km²/yr over the first year after logging (O'Loughlin 1981, Pers. Comm.).

There are several examples of good research on this topic in the United States that add to evidence that the way wood products are removed from the forest is the greatest determinant of whether significantly increased stream sediment will occur, and, if it does, how large the effect will be under given conditions of slope, geology, soils, and rainfall pattern. Megahan (1976) summarized the general results of United States studies up to 1976 in a table presented here as Table 10. In the narrative accompanying this table, he stated:

> No increases in sediment production were recorded in the first group of studies in the table. Except for one study in Alaska, little or no accelerated erosion was noted. Whether low inherent erosion hazards or careful logging methods held down sedimentation cannot be determined conclusively, but special precautions were taken to minimize accelerated erosion. In Alaska, considerable erosion, especially mass erosion, occurred. But there, the particular geomorphic situation prevented almost all of the eroded material from entering the drainage system.
>
> The second group includes three studies of areas where sediment production was accelerated, but was not directly related to increased surface and mass erosion rates. In all cases, however, increased erosion was implied in the reports.
>
> Sedimentation increased and erosion was documented in the last group of seven studies. Erosion from roads was reported more frequently than erosion from cutting and skidding.

Once logging has ceased, unless continuously producing sediment areas have been created such as from landslips or stream banks, sediment rates soon return to preharvesting levels. In Malaysia, Peh (1978) studied adjacent watersheds, one of undisturbed transitional lowland to hill dipterocarp forest and one of "altered," newly regenerated forest. He reported

Table 10. Summary of Studies of the Effect of Logging on Erosion and Sedimentation in the United States

Study Location	Accel. Sediment Production		Location and Type Accelerated Erosion					Comments
			Cut + Skid		Roads			
	Yes	No	Surf. Eros.	Mass Eros.	Surf. Eros.	Mass Eros.	Not Defined	
N.C.		X					X	Cutting only; no roads, no skidding
Mich.		X					X	
Colo.		X			X			Slight road erosion, no sediment to streams
Wash.		X					X	Sediment not discernible
Oreg.		X					X	Sediment not discernible
Alaska		X		X	X			No significant sediment increase
Oreg.		X					X	Regional, statistical study
Calif.		X					X	Regional, statistical study
Colo.		X					X	
Calif.	X							Mostly from channel encroachment
Idaho	X		X		X			Accelerated sed. some drainages, none in others
N.C.	X		X		X			
W. Va.	X		X		X			Varied with care in logging
Oreg.	X		X		X	X		Cut + skid erosion due to slash burning
Oreg.	X		X		X	X		
Idaho	X		X		X	X		

Source: After Megahan (1976).

that despite the altered nature of the vegetation cover, rates of sediment transport were not significantly different from those of undisturbed rainforest. While these rates were not in streams, but rather in tanks from surface wash, they are indicative of the nature of this important component of stream sedimentation.

The effectiveness of streamside buffer strips has been mentioned previously for Queensland conditions in the logging effect studies by Gilmour (1971) and Gilmour et al. (1982). This also has been well illustrated in work by Graynoth (1979) in New Zealand, who reported mean suspended sediment concentrations in mg/1 of 8, 213, 188 and 27 for four respective forest watersheds that had received the following treatments: control, logged with no protection, logged with no protection, and logged with riparian protection. Observations of serious stream sediment problems in South Africa following logging led Bosch and Hewlett (1980) to develop strong recommendations and planning design aids for what they termed "streamside management zones."

NUTRIENT OUTFLOW

Harvesting of commercial wood affects chemical nutrient cycling by changing the amount in storage and modifying the biological arrangements and functions of the soils and forest streams. Also, changes in microclimate due to forest cutting will affect biological activity, rates of oxidation and rates of leaching. Any detachment of soil particles and transport to streams carries attached nutrients into streams. If there is burning of the slash, there is increased volatilization and mineralization of elements bound in organic material. Burning also affects biological activity and microclimate.

Perhaps the most widely known research on the effects of forest harvesting on nutrient cycling, and in particular on nutrient outflow from a monitored catchment, is that conducted at Hubbard Brook Experimental Forest in the northeastern United States (Likens et al. 1970). All trees, saplings, and shrubs on a 15.6 ha watershed were cut and limbed but not removed. No roads were installed. While this was in no sense an example of commercial wood harvesting, it did serve to determine the effect of forest cutting on nutrient outflow. Vegetation regrowth was inhibited for two years by periodic application of herbicides, but allowances were made for the chemical input of these materials. Large increases in streamwater concentration for all major ions except NH_4+, SO_4- and HCO_3- were observed (Likens et al. 1970). The nitrate concentration in the stream exceeded the health levels recommended for drinking water. Stream acidity changed from pH 5.1 to 4.3, a fivefold increase. Bormann and Likens (1981), in summarizing results from this and other Hubbard Brook work, pointed out that loss of dissolved substances not only represents a loss of nutrients from the eco-

Table 11. Nutrient Outputs (kg/ha) in Maimai Watersheds M6 (Undisturbed Control), M7, and M9 During First Two Years After Logging and Burning

Watershed	Year	PO_4-P	NO_3-N	Na	K	Mg	Ca
M6	1978	0.11	0.51	28.25	3.19	3.33	6.29
M7	1977	0.57	2.25	67.37	75.36	21.78	59.18
M7	1978	0.35	10.44	58.72	35.42	21.97	44.81
M9	1977	0.14	1.26	50.13	14.01	9.97	17.12
M9	1978	0.38	5.97	56.93	23.84	11.95	24.62

Source: O'Loughlin et al. (1980).

system, but it also has an environmental impact on aquatic systems draining the cutover forest. They went on to suggest that as long as clearcuts are limited to small areas (several hectares) and the cut area forms a small part of a larger forested watershed, biotic activities in streamwater, plus dilution by water from uncut forests will tend to minimize environmental impacts. Clearcutting on steep slopes or thin soils can lead to long-term changes in structure, metabolism, and biogeochemistry of the forest ecosystem.

Elsewhere in the temperate zone, in actual logging of forested catchments, additional evidence of increased nutrient outflow has been obtained. In New Zealand, O'Loughlin et al. (1980) studied a control, undisturbed forest catchment and two adjacent clearfelled, logged-and-burned catchments, with the results shown in Table 11. In another logged catchment where skyline logging and a protective streamside buffer strip were retained, the increases in nutrient outflow were much less than in the conventionally logged catchments (O'Loughlin 1981, Pers. Comm.).

At Coweeta (U.S.), Swank and Douglass (1977) reported that export of NO_3-N increased for periods up to 20 years following cutting of forest, both with or without removing the products. In Taiwan, the average concentrations of dissolved Ca, Mg, Na, and NO_3-N were higher following clearcutting than from an undisturbed watershed, and since the water yield increased by 50 percent over the control, the total loss of nutrients was substantial (Lin 1981, Pers. Comm.).

No studies were found from monitored catchments in the tropics on the effects of commercial wood harvesting on the nutrient input into discharging streams. It is thought that in the tropical rainforest the disruptions in the tight nutrient cycling pattern and the change in the microclimate and in the biological activity would be even more dramatic than in the temperate zone. This would probably result in greater nutrient outflow following cutting of the forest. Certainly the removal of woody biomass in logging substantially depletes the nutrient budget, for large amounts of nutrients are contained in the boles of the trees. A process like logging removes much of both the nutrient stores and the main nutrient pathways (Golley et al. 1978).

SUMMARY AND IMPLICATIONS

Generalizations about the effects of harvesting commercial wood products are indeed difficult to make because of the many variables listed early in this chapter. Nevertheless, an attempt is made in this section to make some summary statements and to suggest some cause-and-effect relationships so that some policy guidelines may be set forth. Those planning forest development or protection cannot wait until the myriad combinations of natural conditions, timing, harvesting intensity, and logging methods have been researched for tropical forest watersheds.

With the exception of cloud or fog forest situations, forest harvesting seems to result in an increase in height of water table until the regrowing forest has resumed precutting levels of interception and evapotranspiration. Poorly located and dense road and trail networks could result in decreased and more prolonged effects on groundwater levels, and hence on springs and wells.

Streamflow quantity increases throughout the year in response to forest harvesting, with the increase generally in proportion to the amount of canopy removed. The exception to this has occurred following cutting of cloud forests. The effect diminishes rapidly as forest regeneration occurs. The greatest increased percentages in yield occur during the low flow periods. This result has important forest management implications if low flows are a major water resource problem. Stormflow volumes, peak flows and stormflow durations are also *usually* (but not always) increased by harvesting, and these effects may produce upstream flash flooding in, and somewhat downstream of, the logged area. Logging roads, skid trails, and log landings can increase these stormflow parameters further if they are not well planned, well constructed, and well maintained.

These stormflow effects must not be extrapolated to support statements that appear in the press (and the misconception commonly held) that logging in upper watersheds is the principal *cause* of serious and widespread flooding in the lower reaches of major river basins. If the whole basin were to be logged at once, this situation could be true on occasion, but such a situation is unrealistic. Hewlett (1982) has reviewed the relationship between "Forests and Floods in the Light of Recent Investigation." He concludes that forest operations in upstream catchments have not been shown to increase flood flows seriously in major streams. He also suggests that this conclusion is applicable to the tropics as well as the temperate zone, from which has come most of the experimental evidence. Hewlett indicates that the cumulative downstream effects of fairly widespread forest harvesting in a basin can be calculated by streamflow routing techniques, and that they will prove to be minor in comparison with the influences of rainfall and basin storage.

What is referred to previously is the downstream flood peak discharges in the lower basin with respect to forest operations. Mass soil movement and other serious erosional consequences of poor logging may indeed lead to stream sediment problems that can aggravate flooding effects downstream. It must also be remembered that this chapter deals with commercial logging, not with conversion of large areas of upland watershed to overgrazed, compacted, and degraded land; nor to compacted, eroding, and degrading cropland; nor to urbanizing areas with a large percentage of nonabsorbing surface. Under these land uses, there may well be substantially increased flood flow volumes in the lower reaches of rivers.

The increased erosion rates caused by commercial forest harvesting are mainly attributable to the disturbance of the soil by wood extraction techniques, mainly from log landings, skid trails, and roads. On steep slopes and with high intensity rain patterns, the erosion can be quite serious and persist for many years. Logging methods, such as by high-line or helicopter that reduce the amount of soil disturbance, reduce the erosion impact. Minimizing road density and properly locating, constructing, and maintaining roads are important considerations. There exist a number of excellent logging guidelines for reducing the erosion consequences of this form of forest land use.

One further erosion effect, which results from simply cutting the trees and which may occur even with the most careful extraction techniques, results from the reduction of root shear strength. On certain critical slope areas, any forest cutting may initiate mass soil movements. Advance identification of these critical soil areas is possible, and commercial forest harvesting should be excluded from them.

While it is virtually impossible to prevent some increase in erosion from forest harvesting (except on level land), increased stream sediment is not necessarily a consequence of logging. As currently carried out in the tropics, however (and usually in the temperate zone also), logging is usually followed by increased sediment in streams, with its potentially deleterious impacts on aquatic life, reservoir siltation rates, altered stream channels that may increase flooding and reduce navigability, and reduced water quality for domestic and industrial use. Sediment problems can be reduced and even eliminated in some instances, as far as logging impacts are concerned, by a number of sediment control practices. Logging techniques that minimize on-site erosion are important, as mentioned previously. Keeping roads and skid trails out of watercourses, or at least crossing them at right angles using bridges or culverts, are important sediment-reducing actions. The establishment of undisturbed streamside (riparian) buffer zones is of major importance, since such zones not only minimize accelerated streambank erosion, but they also trap much erosion material moving downslope from the logged area above.

Increased nutrient outflow from the logged portion of the watershed is an inevitable consequence of logging, no matter how carefully the extraction is done. Poor harvesting practices can increase the discharge. Minimizing soil movement will minimize nutrient outflow in streams from the disturbed area. In addition to the water export of nutrients from the site, the harvested biomass itself removes a substantial part of the ecosystem budget in the humid tropics. Additional research on this combined loss is needed to properly assess impacts of the trend toward shorter-rotation, total-tree harvesting on the nutrient budgets of tropical forest ecosystems.

Prompt and adequate forest regeneration is the best assurance that any increased erosion rate, sediment effect, and nutrient outflow will return speedily to preharvesting levels. This will be easier to achieve in the moist tropical forest than in the dry forest.

Technical harvesting guidelines have been developed to minimize adverse hydrologic/soil/nutrient effects of logging. A brief summary of such guidelines is presented in Appendix C.

5
Grazing on Forestland

Much of the grazing on tropical and subtropical forestlands is really a conversion of the forest to grazing land. It often involves annual or periodic burning and gradual removal of the trees through nonsustainable fuelwood (or charcoal) cutting or nonsustainable fodder lopping. This pattern of conversion is common in the open woodlands. Another pattern of conversion has been reported by Hamilton (1976). It involves what has been called "shifting (or slash-and-burn) grazing," and may be carried out in closed tropical forests, including moist forests that are not easily burned. This is not a "traditional," stable pattern of land use corresponding to stable shifting agriculture (see Chapter 2), but is a migratory, productivity-degrading land use in which the forest is cleared, burned, grazed for some years and then abandoned, leaving behind a degraded grassland or savanna. The impacts of these *conversion* practices on the hydrologic and soil variables under consideration are treated in the chapter on "Conversion to Grassland" (Chapter 8).

What is considered herein is the practice of grazing in forested areas over a long time, on a more or less sustainable basis. Such a forest grazing system can be (and has been) established in open forest, especially woodland. A critical time in this system comes when the trees begin to deteriorate or require harvesting because of maturity. At such a point, the grazing animals need to be confined (or new seedlings fenced), and fire must be controlled until the forest component of this forest/grass system is reestablished. Such a system represents a true joint-production or multiple-use system in which the net benefit from the two products is greater than the benefit from either single output system. This type of system is often subsumed under many definitions of agroforestry, which have a forestry and a grazing combination.

Usually the forest grazing practice involves domestic animals (cattle, horses, sheep, goats, carabaos, etc.), but in some places substantial herds of native or introduced wildlife herbivores (deer, feral goats, mouflon, etc.) may also be involved. The impact of grazing will depend to a very large extent on the stocking intensity in relation to the carrying capacity of the area and whether the animals use only grass or mainly browse woody material. In this section, we will assume sustainable stocking levels, and consider domesticated grazing animals.

GROUNDWATER, SPRINGS, AND WELLS

There appears to be no quantitative evidence of any effects of forest grazing on groundwater, springs, or wells. It is known that compaction of the soil surface by hooved animals does reduce infiltration rates and thus could affect groundwater accessions negatively (see Table 12). Mott et al. (1979) found that heavy grazing and drought caused soil "seals" in open eucalypt woodlands in northern Australia. About 90 percent of the intense early season rainfall entered soil under grassed areas, but only 25 to 30 percent entered the soil under "seals," leading to locally increased runoff. Effects of grazing on groundwater should be added to watershed grazing research in order to provide answers to this question.

Table 12. Surface Erosion and Infiltration Rates under Pine Forest

			Infiltration Rates	
Slope	**Grazing Treatment (cow/days)**	**Three-Year Erosion Depth (mm)**	**Before Grazing (mm/hr)**	**After Grazing (mm/hr)**
0°–10°	31–40 (light)	15.7	205.1	48.9
	55–70 (heavy)	18.5	200.6	44.5
20°–40°	31–40 (light)	26.1	285.3	137.0
	55–70 (heavy)	40.5	357.4	158.0
Rolling	Not grazed	14.9	365.1	353.9

Source: Adapted from Murai (1973).

STREAMFLOW QUANTITY

Compaction of soil surface results in reduced infiltration, leading to increased runoff, which in turn may lead to increased streamflow. In the study by Mott et al. (1979), the terrain was flat to gently sloping, and the locally increased runoff could have been internally redistributed rather than appearing as increased streamflow (no streamflow measurements were made). In the humid southeastern United States, one 49-ha forest watershed at Coweeta was grazed by six cattle for four months per year for 11 years with no water yield changes noted (Douglass 1981).

TIMING AND DISTRIBUTION OF STREAMFLOW

Uncontrolled forest grazing is thought to cause irregular stream flow (usually reduced low flows) in the northern part of the Philippines (Saplaco 1981, Pers. Comm.). No experimental evidence of the effects of forest grazing on the timing of streamflow resulted from the Coweeta study (Douglass 1981).

ON-SITE EROSION

Where a good grass cover is maintained between the trees, no serious erosion should occur. In the Coweeta grazing experiment, if sheet erosion occurred, it did not show up as increased turbidity in the stream during the first eight years of the study (Douglass 1981). This was the case in spite of the tendency for the animals to congregate near the stream, where ostensibly their trampling might have led to stream-bank erosion. However, after eight years, higher turbidities occurred during storm periods, probably due to the cumulative soil compaction, reduced infiltration, and greater exposure of soil.

Erosion occurs when stocking is too great to maintain the forage cover. This is confirmed by the data presented by Murai (1973) (see Table 12). These data, which also show the effect of increasing slope, were compiled after three years of grazing treatment. Studies by Masrur and Hanif (1972) in Pakistan illustrate the gradient from forest to overgrazing, with reports of relative soil loss on steep slopes of 1:20:80 for chir pine forest, protected grass cover, and depleted grass cover, respectively.

SEDIMENT IN STREAMS

Aside from the Coweeta study, there is little evidence available to show any increased sediment yields in streams from sustainable grazing in forestlands. However, if overstocking occurs and bare ground is exposed, the lack of vegetative cover plus the increased runoff resulting from compaction will produce this effect without question. The empirical, if not experimental, evidence is present in overgrazed, deteriorated forests in upper watersheds throughout the tropics. For instance, it is reported that the overgrazed mountainous watershed of the Bermejo River, a tributary of the Paraguay River in Argentina, contributes 80 percent of the 100 million tons of sediment a year deposited near Buenos Aires, though it constitutes only 4 percent of the Parana watershed (Pereira 1972).* Similar situations have been observed but not researched in the Himalayan arc for the major rivers of the Indian subcontinent. These are hardly forestlands any more; they are now converted lands. Douglas (1967) in tropical Australia compared steep forested headwater streams with less steep, lower rainfall,

---

*One might also look for differences in parent material and soils to explain this phenomenon, but no information was presented other than that reported.

54

lower reaches of the same stream that were mainly in grazing land use and found increased sediment loads in the lower reaches.

NUTRIENT OUTFLOW

There is no available information on changes in nutrient outflow due to grazing in forests. The likely effect would be an increase, since the tendency is for livestock to harvest nutrients and move them downhill as they defecate and urinate on their way to water. The tendency for animals to congregate at water supply areas would heighten this effect.

SUMMARY AND IMPLICATIONS

If the stocking level is limited to the carrying capacity of the forest so that the forage cover is maintained, there seems to be little effect on any of the variables considered, with the possible exception of nutrient outflow. That is a very big "if." Such control is difficult to achieve either on private land or on public land being grazed under permit. Moreover, for the area to be maintained as forest grazing land, there is a need for extraordinary measures to secure adequate replacement of the tree component when the mature trees are harvested, through natural regeneration or artificial planting. Trees must be protected by fencing during the early establishment period. Without control, overgrazing will produce increased runoff, increased erosion and sediment yield, and probably increases in stormflows.

Forest areas that provide municipal water supplies should not be grazed, or if this is not feasible due to lack of jurisdiction, at least a riparian buffer strip with no grazing should be established. In addition, the water must be given special treatment to render it safe.

Wild animals at certain densities will resemble livestock in their impacts, and their numbers may have to be controlled by hunting to keep them within the carrying capacity.

With respect to the use of periodic controlled burning as a tool to maintain forage/forest balance, Chapter 6 indicates some of the impacts of fire on the variables considered in this report.

In certain circumstances, where open woodland is the natural vegetation type, forest grazing may be a sustainable use of land and have no serious adverse consequences on watershed characteristics—if the stocking and distribution of animals is controlled.

6
Burning Forestland

Fire can be an important forest management tool or a destructive agent of change. Prescribed burning by skilled land managers can change vegetative cover to a desired state rapidly and cheaply, without detrimental on-site or off-site effects. Wildfires, however, can severely damage the forest resource and significantly impair the products and services that forest ecosystems provide. This chapter will not deal with burning of slash following harvest cutting of forests as part of a regeneration or site preparation for planting procedure.

In the *humid* tropics, the natural evergreen hardwood forests do not normally burn, though the edges may be "nibbled" from adjacent altered land where fire is used. However, in an unusually dry season the litter may support fire. Following logging, when the slash has dried somewhat, fire may be started in the slash. Young hardwood plantations that have not closed and still have grass cover are also susceptible to burning. Other forests in the tropics will burn during the dry season.

GROUNDWATER, SPRINGS, AND WELLS

There have been few studies directly measuring the effect of fires in the forest on the water table. A prescribed burn that is restricted to the forest floor, perhaps killing seedlings but leaving the main tree canopy intact, is not thought to have any effect on the water table. Uncontrolled wildfire may have an effect; however, two countervailing influences appear to be important with fires that are hot or prolonged and that kill trees. By killing trees, the canopy is reduced, permitting greater throughfall and reducing evapotranspiration losses, which could account for increased accessions to groundwater. Megahan (1981, Pers. Comm.) reports an increase in the base flow component of the hydrograph following fire in a *Pinus ponderosa* stand in the western United States. Similar results have apparently been obtained in some Australian studies (Boughton 1981, Pers. Comm.).

On the other hand, surface sealing of the soil has occurred after fire in the Philippines, the extent of sealing depending on soil type and fire temperature. This reduced infiltration and percolation into groundwater aquifers (Costales 1979). Fire has made some soils nonwettable (hydrophobic), thus leading to increased runoff and reduced infiltration (Dyrness 1967). Further research is needed on the effects of fire on groundwater.

STREAMFLOW QUANTITY

The impact of burning on annual water yield appears to vary depending on such site factors as soil type, slope, amount of litter consumed, whether or not trees were killed, and how great a percentage of the cover canopy was affected.

Where only the forest floor is affected, as in prescribed burning or a light wildfire in a deciduous forest, plot studies often show increased runoff, but watershed experiments measuring streamflow have in at least one instance shown no effect on water yield (Douglass 1981). This result at Coweeta (United States) was from a single burn in a mountain watershed.

Wildfires are a different matter. In Australia, they have been shown to increase streamflow yield by 43 to 235 percent (McArthur 1964; McArthur and Cheney 1965). Following an accidental burn in Japan, Nakano (1971) found an annual water yield increase of around 23 to 26 percent. Toebes and Goh (1975) in Malaysia reported a 10-percent increase in average annual runoff after forest burning. However, in Australia following one of Victoria's most serious wildfires, Langford (1974) reported no significant difference in streamflow for 5 years after the fire, and then reported a decrease—over the following 21 years, streamflow was 24 percent below the average before the fire. He attributed the difference in water yield to an increase in evapotranspiration of the young *Eucalyptus regnans* regrowth. This study stands in contrast to all of the others.

TIMING AND DISTRIBUTION OF STREAMFLOW

There is little experimental evidence of changes in the timing of flow from light fires, as in a controlled burn. Where there is severe wildfire with reduced infiltration, increased surface flow would seem to cause higher flood peaks and reduced time to peaking. Pereira, in a working group report, has documented major increases in flood peaks—approximately five times the expected flow—following uncontrolled fire in two catchments in Australia's Snowy Mountains region (UNESCO 1969). Numerous studies in the western United States, particularly California, reported large increases in stormflows following wildfire on forestlands (Megahan 1982, Pers. Comm.).

ON-SITE EROSION

Moderate and light fires have very little effect on soil properties, including erodibility, according to Dyrness (1967), who examined the existing evidence of the effects of burning on erosion in the western United States. On the other hand, he cited studies showing significant increases in erosion following severe burning. Douglass (1981) confirmed the former situation from work at Coweeta and suggested that rapid recovery of vegetation after a light fire is a most important factor. Following a fire in a Hawaiian watershed, Wood et al. (1969) found no evidence of widespread erosion, and reported that six months afterward, 94 percent of the survey transect length had a vegetation density of greater than 50 percent. Fireweed (*Erechtites hieracifolia*) was the dominant recovery species.

Repeated annual burning and wildfire each has different effects. Rowe (1941) studied the impacts of burning in the woodland-chapparal-grass type forest of the United States over a nine-year period. He found that the unburned plots had no erosion, that plots burned over twice in nine years lost an average of 10 t/ha, and that plots burned annually averaged a loss of 279 t/ha. In Pakistan, frequently burned stands of chir pine (*Pinus roxburghii*) are reported to exhibit as much erosion as unterraced croplands (Raeder-Roitzsch and Masur 1968).

In one study in Japan, a wildfire burned one slope that had just been logged and another that had been logged four years previously. Six months after burning, a heavy storm caused extensive erosion on the recently logged slope, but not on the partially revegetated one (Tsukamoto and Kimura 1976). The reason suggested was that root networks held the soil together.

Dramatic increases in the amount and concentration of stream sediment were reported for catchments in the Snowy Mountains of Australia (UNESCO 1969) following wildfire. These increases must be attributed at least partly to an increase in on-site erosion as well as stream erosion (see following section on sediment in streams).

It appears that the most important fire-caused changes in the soil erosion rate are not in the mineral soil itself, but in the removal of the vegetation and litter that protects the surface. This is a function of fire intensity, speed of fire movement over an area, and the periodicity of burning.

SEDIMENT IN STREAMS

In Malaysian land development projects, large-scale forest cutting accompanied by burnings has led to so much sediment production that small stream channels have been obliterated and large stream channels modified (Low and Leigh 1972). Such large-scale changes in areas of low gradient raise the river beds and may seriously aggravate flooding. Brown (1972), in a study of a bushfire in a forested catchment in New South Wales, Australia, reports that for four to five years after the fire, the streams carried greatly increased sediment loads, but that after that time the hydrologic characteristics returned to a preburn status. One of the best documented and most dramatic reports of the effect of fire has been presented in a UNESCO report by the Working Group on the Influence of Man on the Hydrologic Cycle (1972):

> An instructive example of the effects of fires on water supply is provided by the experience of the Snowy Mountains Hydro-Electric Authority in the Australian Alps. Here a major uncontrollable forest fire in inaccessible rugged country burned out the catchment areas of Wallace's Creek and the Yarrangobilly River, of 41 and 224 km², respectively. These catchments had been gauged for some eight years previously, with detailed sampling of suspended soil load. After the fire the flow pattern changed abruptly, with sharp flow peaks from the burned-out areas. Rainstorms, which from previous records would have been expected to give rise to flows of 60–80 m³/sec (cumecs), produced a peak of 370 cumecs. The suspended sediment content at a flow of 60–80 cumecs has been increased by 100 times in comparison with the soil content before the fire. A storm occurring some seven months after the fire gave the highest sediment concentration recorded at Wallace's Creek. At a flow of 95 cumecs the concentration was 14.4 percent by weight, equivalent to 115,000 tons per day. This concentration is high by world standards. On the same day the River Yarrangobilly, with a flow of 47 cumecs, yielded an equivalent sediment load of 45,000 tons per day. The Snowy Mountains Hydro-Electric Authority estimates from the increased flow rate and increased sediment concentration that the total sediment load in Wallace's Creek is probably 1,000 times greater than it was before the fire.

By contrast, Boughton (1970) reports that following the severe fire in November 1968, no erosion or increase in turbidity was experienced in the Chichester (Australia) catchment providing Newcastle's water supply. The fire burned about 20 percent of the catchment in the region, especially in the area immediately around the dam. There were no heavy rains for more than six months following the fire, giving ground vegetation an opportunity to become reestablished without the occurrence of erosion or severe floods. This illustrates the importance of weather pattern in the period immediately after a fire. It is another factor to consider in estimating the effects of a severe burn.

NUTRIENT OUTFLOW

One might expect that burning would mineralize at least some of the organic fraction of the surface soils, and that runoff containing ash and leachate would increase the nutrient loads of the streams. Particularly in a severe burn, which kills trees, it is to be expected that the kind of nutrient outflow obtained at Hubbard Brook (U.S.) following cutting (Likens et al. 1970) would occur. However, at Coweeta, Douglass (1981, Pers. Comm.) found no significant changes in nutrient outflow from single intense burns in deciduous forests. In a replicated prescribed burning test in the Piedmont (eastern U.S.), four pine-covered watersheds were burned twice without changing the export of NO_3-N, PO_4-P, NH_4-N, Ca, Mg, Na, and K (Douglass and Van Lear, in press).

SUMMARY AND IMPLICATIONS

The impact of burning forested lands on the water-soil nutrient factors considered in this report is not well research. Unquestionably, much depends on fire intensity, length of time, and the frequency of occurrence in a given watershed area. The speed of revegetation has much to do with any increase in erosion, sedimentation, nutrient outflow, water yield, and any effect on streamflow timing. Thus in humid areas where revegetation occurs promptly, the effects of fire, even of wildfire, are minimized. In drier areas, where vegetation regrowth may be slower, the effects could be more prolonged and serious. Little is known about the effects on groundwater, springs, and wells. Significant increases in water yield can occur where trees are killed; they will persist until the evapotranspiration rate has returned to normal. Replacement of a mature or overmature forest by a vigorous postfire regrowth could reduce water yields.

There seems to be no compelling hydrologic reason for prohibiting the use of prescribed burning in watersheds if it is carefully executed.

7
Conversion to Forest Tree Plantations

Following the harvesting of original natural forest in tropical developing countries, one option for subsequent use of the land is to reforest the cutover area artificially. This often leads to more rapid tree regeneration. Also, the new tree crop species can be one or more that have high commercial value and grow rapidly, thus making the forest more useful to society. There is much controversy over this practice, especially when the conversion involves the extreme case of replacing complex, primary lowland rainforest with a monoculture of an exotic tree species on relatively large areas of land. When considering the benefits (increased value, shorter rotation, easier management, etc.) and the costs (higher pest and disease risk, loss of species locally, major habitat change for wildlife, reduced usefulness to traditional peoples, etc.), the effects on water, soil, and nutrient loss also should be considered.

This chapter will consider the hydrologic/soil effects of converting tropical forested watershed to forest tree plantations. The effects of establishing forest tree plantations on land already deforested for some time are discussed in Chapter 12, "Reforestation or Afforestation." Most of the forestland currently being planted each year is of the latter type (reforestation or afforestation of open land), but there are also substantial areas of conversion taking place, including well-known examples in Brazil (Jari), Indonesia (East Kalimantan), and Papua New Guinea (Gogol). Moreover, as Whitmore (1981) points out, the potential of intensive plantation silviculture to reduce the wood deficits in many Latin American nations augurs for more of this type of conversion rather than less, in spite of the recognized drawbacks. This may well be true for Africa and the Asian-Pacific regions as well. However, as the amount of natural forest in a nation dwindles, at some point the recognition of the loss of cultural heritage and values associated with native forest becomes overwhelming, and conversion, especially using exotics, becomes rare. This practice is currently being heatedly debated in Australia, and, following much controversy and study, New Zealand has formulated a conservative policy with respect to conversion of its remaining indigenous forests (New Zealand Forest Service 1977).

The hydrologic/soil effects of converting natural forests to plantations depend on how different they are from each other in such characteristics as seasonal foliage response (whether deciduous or evergreen during the dry or cool season) and crown density and shape. They will also depend on whether or not any disturbance, such as site preparation, is associated with the planting activity. One reason for converting to forest plantations is to permit more intensive management and more frequent harvests. These practices require more frequent installation and maintenance of road and skidding networks, which affect the hydrologic and soil processes in the watershed. Many of the effects on soil and water, therefore, are not simply because the kind of forest is different, but because of the disturbance that accompanies the conversion process. It is difficult to handle these complicating factors in an orderly fashion.

Conversion to tree plantations is usually preceded by clearcutting. The effects of clearcutting are dealt with in Chapter 4, "Harvesting Commercial Wood," and these temporary effects would have to be factored into any assessment of total effects. In a few cases, burning may be used to remove debris that would interfere with the planting operation. What is known or surmised about the effects of such burning have been dealt with in Chapter 6.

GROUNDWATER, SPRINGS, AND WELLS

The effects on the water table in the tropics, or indeed in the temperate zone, of replacing natural forest with forest plantations have not been sufficiently studied to permit conclusive statements to be made. Most observers are inclined to support Wicht (1949), who has stated that plantations of exotics require the same amount of water as indigenous forest under South African conditions. One would therefore expect the changes in springs and wells to be minimal. However, from the mountainous areas of Java, Indonesia, came qualitative information that water levels in wells under developing plantations of *Pinus merkusii* are lower than those under native forest (Manan 1981, Pers. Comm.). Rouysungnern (1981, Pers. Comm.) has suggested that in northern Thailand, groundwater recharge under native forest is less than recharge under pine plantations, which generally have shown smaller interception losses. In central North Island, New Zealand, in porous pumice soils, Knight and Will (1977) have shown in lysimeter studies that after 12 years of growth, a young *Pinus radiata* stand reduced the quantity of deep seepage beyond the rooting zone by 163 mm per year. These results do not support Wicht's statement, but Pereira's work comparing Monterey cypress and radiata pine with native bamboo forest in East Africa generally *does* support Wicht (Pereira and Hosegood 1962). Edwards and Blackie (1981) have reported that converting native bamboo forest to plantations of *P. patula* initially decreased water use, but that once the pine canopy had closed, no significant differences in groundwater recharge were detectable in the East African catchments.

The picture is far from clear because of the variables involved and because good studies directly measuring changes in water table levels or effects on wells and springs are lacking.

STREAMFLOW QUANTITY

Fortunately, some good data have been generated on how converting natural forest to tree plantations affects water yield, though not very many of the possible combinations have been studied. The immediate effects of removal of the native forest have already been discussed in Chapter 4; there has invariably been a marked increase in streamflow quantity. The duration of the major increase seems to depend on how long it takes before a closed-canopy forest again occupies the site. Reforestation can hasten this process when compared with natural regeneration, although in the more humid tropics, natural regrowth may be about as rapid and dense.

Aside from this removal effect, there are some differences in water yield that are attributable to the change in the kind of forest. Most experiments have involved a conversion from broadleaved and usually deciduous natural forest to coniferous, needle-leaved, evergreen forest, conditions under which the effects would be most pronounced. As the replacement plantation moves closer to the original forest in crown characteristics, the effects expected would be less. Most studies have shown at least a slight decrease in streamflow resulting from conversion.

Australian experience, however, has indicated little or no change in yield, mainly from conversion of native eucalypt forest to *Pinus radiata*. Results from conversion of 11 catchments ranging in size from 4 to 300 ha indicated no differences between species (Bell and Gatenby 1969). Boughton (1970), in summarizing the state of knowledge as of 1970 for the Australian Water Resources Council, reported: "All evidence supports the proposition that there is negligible difference in water yield between species of *mature* forest. When native eucalypt forest is cleared to establish an exotic pine plantation, there is likely to be an increase in the amount of water yield while the pine forest is immature and has not established its full root depth, and this difference should disappear as the trees mature." This agrees with Wicht's statement about South Africa reported earlier (Wicht 1949).

Only slight differences are reported from New Zealand where indigenous *evergreen* forest has been converted to radiata pine. Pearce and Rowe (1979) indicated that interception and transpiration losses were comparable under these conditions, that annual streamflow yields would be decreased by no more than 200 mm, and that under most soil and rainfall conditions the decrease was unlikely to be more than 100 mm.

64

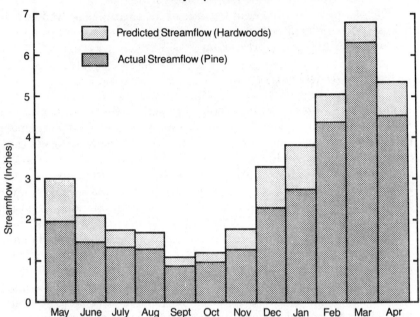

Figure 9. Decrease in streamflow over a year following conversion of broadleaved (hardwood) forest to pine (*Pinus strobus*) at Coweeta (U.S.). (Courtesy U.S. Forest Service)

However, such small differences are not manifest where there is a dormant season characterized by deciduousness in the natural forest, and where it is replaced by an evergreen forest. At Coweeta in the southeastern United States, replacement of mixed, deciduous, broadleaved forest with *Pinus strobus* produced marked differences (see Figure 9). A rapid decline in yield occurred to about age 13, then a slower decline, till currently at age 25, the streamflow is 20 to 25 cm (20 percent) less than when the watershed had its indigenous forest cover (Swank and Miner 1968, Swank and Douglass 1974). Largest reductions occurred in the dormant season and were attributed primarily to greater interception losses by the pine (Helvey 1967). Process modeling studies, however, indicated that the reduction may be about equally attributed to an increase in transpiration and interception (Swift et al. 1975). Catchment studies done in Australia have also found that the streamflow from 13- to 22-year-old radiata pine plantations was only 3.5 percent of the rainfall, substantially lower than from comparable eucalypt forests (King 1981, Pers. Comm.). Thinning of the pine, however, increased streamflow to 12 percent of the rainfall.

TIMING AND DISTRIBUTION OF STREAMFLOW

The only data available on timing of streamflow come from watersheds at Coweeta in the United States, where deciduous broadleaved forest was converted to white pine (*P. strobus*). After age 15, flow from the pine forest was less than that from the original forest during every month of the year, with the largest reductions in the dormant season and occasionally exceeding 3 cm/month (Swank and Douglass 1974). Flow distribution also changed, with low flows being reduced 10 to 20 percent overall; the change in low flow is least during the dormant season and greatest during the growing season (Helvey and Douglass 1971). Douglass (1981, Pers. Comm.) stated that the last analysis of stormflow volumes was made when the pines were 10 to 13 years of age, and no change in stormflow volumes was apparent. He expected that further study would show that since total flow has been reduced by 25 to 30 percent, stormflow volumes and peaks would be significantly reduced compared to the original hardwood cover.

ON-SITE EROSION

Conversion of natural forests to forest plantations appears to result in a wide range of on-site erosion responses, depending on the nature of the site preparation, for any given combination of topography, soil, and climate.

In Fiji (Drysdale 1981, Pers. Comm.) and Puerto Rico (Whitmore 1981, Pers. Comm.), techniques such as partial cutting followed by planting, then removal of the residual native trees by girdling or poisoning, reduced the impacts of plantation establishment on erosion rates.

In Indonesia the replacement of native forests with legume plantations resulted in high initial erosion rates on steep slopes (over 100t/ha/yr), but after the plantations were well established and a litter layer had formed erosion rates declined to preconversion levels (Manan 1981, Pers. Comm.).

The effects of conversion of tropical moist forests to plantations of exotic pines (*Pinus caribaea*) have been studied in a series of 22 small catchments at three locations in Queensland, Australia (Cassells et al. 1982). This well-designed study considered the effects of clearing, the effects of land treatment for establishment, and the effects as the plantations age on sediment concentrations following different treatments over time. The three locations represented coastal lowland rainforest, undulating headwaters, and elevated plateau country, all in tropical and subtropical climates. In general, there was little increase in erosion where establishment took place without mechanical cultivation. Where ploughing was used, erosion occurred, in some cases not only sheet erosion but extensive gullying. Contour strip ploughing showed less erosion than broadcast ploughing. Erosion rates returned to preconversion levels rapidly after the establishment phase was over, unless the cultivation disturbance had exposed unstable stream banks (in which case these areas continued to erode well into the plantation rotation). Planting without cultivation had little effect on erosion rates. The study suggests that increases in erosion due to conversion can be minimized by avoiding cultivation where that is possible, and that where it is not, contour strip ploughing techniques can be used effectively.

The effects of land-clearing methods for establishing forest plantations in Nigeria have been summarized by Ball (1981). For moist lowland forest, most conversions are to *Gmelina arborea, Tectona grandis, Terminalia ivorensis, Nauclea diderrichii* and mahoganies. The common method of mechanized clearing is knockdown by shearing with a tractor cutting blade, windrowing with rakes or blades into rows 50 m apart, and burning the windrow. Compared with manual methods using chainsaws and burning (no windrowing), sheet erosion was greatly increased and soil compaction occurred. Ball feels that mechanical clearing must replace manual clearing to meet Nigeria's wood needs, but that methods have to be developed for minimizing erosion. On the other hand, Sanchez (1981) has reported that in the massive conversion to plantations of *Gmelina arborea, Pinus caribaea,* and *Eucalyptus deglupta* that occurred at Jari in Brazil's Amazon, bulldozer clearing was abandoned in favor of slash-and-burn clearing because of problems with soil compaction, topsoil displacement, and possible nutrient losses.

Once the plantations have become established, most evidence is in agreement with the Australian work of Cassells et al. (1982), namely, that conversion per se does not significantly affect erosion rates one way or the other, since so much depends on the topography, the soils, and the nature of the precipitation (for example, Edwards and Blackie 1981). Saplaco and Perino (1981, Pers. Comm.) have indicated that in the Philippines, overland flow and surface erosion are least with plantations of *Abizia falcataria* and increase slightly in the following order: secondary regrowth of dipterocarps, virgin dipterocarp forests, and *Anthocephalus chinensis* plantations. However, there are special circumstances that prohibit generalization. Bell (1973) has reported significant erosion problems in pure teak (*Tectona grandis*) plantations in Trinidad, and similar observations have been made in El Salvador and Thailand (Kunkle in press). Michaelson (1975) has suggested that the erosion problem with teak may be solved by including a legume tree such as *Leucaena leucocephala* or *Acacia glauca.*

SEDIMENT IN STREAMS

What seems the best evidence of the effects of forest conversion to tree plantations comes from the Queensland studies (Cassells et al. 1982). The low sediment yields were from catchments that did not involve cultivation as part of site preparation for planting, or that were older, established plantations. "Establishment without cultivation had no measurable impact on stream sedimentation in this particular environment [open forest pockets interspersed with tropical rainforests on elevated hinterland with a marked summer wet season and an average rainfall of 2,060 mm]." Where cultivation was used in the catchments, the retention of buffer strips of undisturbed native vegetation along the watercourses markedly reduced sedimentation impacts. Where clearing and/or site preparation resulted in bare, unstable stream banks, these areas continued to act as sediment sources well into the life of the established plantation. Where ploughing was involved, contour strip ploughing reduced erosion and resulted in less sediment.

In summarizing the New Zealand experience with conversion to *P. radiata* and the U.S. experience at Coweeta in converting to *P. strobus*, both O'Loughlin (1981, Pers. Comm.) and Douglass (1981, Pers. Comm.), respectively, indicate that sediment yields from maturing plantations are no different than yields from indigenous forest. O'Loughlin, for instance, cites unpublished data from 23-year-old plantations indicating average yields of around 25 m³/km² in small catchments, which are very similar to data from two control catchments in native forest. Douglass indicates that because of road construction in one converted watershed, a mass failure of about 0.1 ha did contribute sediment to the stream until stabilized. He intuitively believes that the physical stability of both soil and channel has somewhat increased under the pine forest due to the reductions in flow obtained (see "Streamflow Quantity").

NUTRIENT OUTFLOW

The initial activity in converting native forest to forest tree plantations is the felling of the forest. As discussed in Chapter 4, most studies have shown a sharp increase in nutrient outflow (particularly nitrogen) following clearfelling, with a return to the previous status as revegetation occurs. Unfortunately, these results are mainly from temperate zone watershed studies. There are no good reasons, however, why the same processes should not occur in the tropics, resulting in sharp increases in nutrient outflow when this nutrient cycling system is broken, especially in the *humid* tropics where high-precipitation leaching and increased oxidation are more intense.

Once the conversion has occurred, however, the nutrient outflow may not be very different than it was under the natural forest. Conversion of broadleaved forests to conifers probably represents the extreme case, and the evidence, at least from temperate zone research, indicates small differences. The early results from a number of New Zealand catchment studies have indicated that concentrations and outputs of dissolved nutrients (N

Table 13. Comparison of the Concentrations of Total Phosphorus (TP) and NO$_3$ –N in Stream Water (mg/l)

Concentration	Exotic Forest		Indigenous Forest	
	TP	NO$_3$–N	TP	NO$_3$–N
Maximum	0.76	2.40	0.64	2.40
95 Percentile	0.17	0.93	0.09	0.74
Median	0.04	0.10	0.02	0.05

Source: Adapted from Cooke (1980).

Table 14. Mean Concentrations of Elements in Streamwater Draining Small Catchments (mg/l)

Element	Exotic Pine Forest	Indigenous Forest
PO$_4$-P	0.04	0.02
NO$_3$-N	0.06	0.03
NH$_4$	0.01	0.02
Na	c.4.10	2.29
K	0.70	0.48
Mg	0.50	0.27
Ca	1.60	0.93

Source: O'Loughlin (1981, Pers. Comm.).

and P) in streamwater are only marginally higher from maturing radiata pine plantations than from undisturbed indigenous beech-podocarp mixed hardwood forests (O'Loughlin 1981, Pers. Comm.).

The concentrations were somewhat higher in 12 catchment studies dealing with total phosphorous and NO$_3$ – N (nutrients of importance in eutrophication), as shown by Cooke (1980) in his summary of water quality data. His analysis is summarized in Table 13.

O'Loughlin (1981, Pers. Comm.) has provided additional unpublished material from a converted catchment study in northwestern South Island (Table 14).

On the other hand, Swank and Douglass (1977) have reported that though the ion concentration at Coweeta remained the same, the reduced streamflow experienced in the pine watersheds meant an export of 1 to nearly 4 kg/ha/yr less (40 to 75 percent less) of Mg, K, Ca, and Na than their controls. In spite of the NO$_3$ – N concentration in the streamflow being greater, the decreased streamflow meant that the outflow total was not greatly different.

One tropical situation study available from Queensland, Australia has implications relating to this process. Brasell et al. (1980), in studying mineral element content and quantity of litterfall under tropical rainforest and a plantation of *Araucaria cunninghamii*, found that there was little difference in annual accession to the soil of N, P, Na, K, and Ca. Therefore, if streamflows are not markedly different between the original and the converted forest (the general experience and prevailing thinking in tropical Australia), the nutrient outflow should not be greatly different.

One can only speculate, however, on what may occur under a regime of clearfelling plantations of fast-growing, short-rotation forests for energy, involving whole tree (and branches) removal. (See, for instance, work by Bruijnzeel [1982] with *Agathis loranthifolia* plantations in Java and his speculations about short-rotation, total-tree harvesting.) The possible nutrient budget reductions due to export of the biomass from the site would undoubtedly result in (1) higher outflows in the stream water, more frequently at the harvest times, and (2) gradually decreasing nutrient outflows from the maturing plantations over successive rotations.

SUMMARY AND IMPLICATIONS

The counteracting of conservation and development forces in the policy arena will undoubtedly keep very much alive the issue of whether or not to convert a dwindling indigenous forest estate to forest tree plantations, especially to exotic, single-species plantations. The increasing need for wood energy, as well as the need to make forest lands more economically productive, pushes in the direction of more conversions with fast-growing planted trees. Those who oppose widespread conversions point out the increasingly important biological, aesthetic, recreational, and heritage values of the remaining native forests, and wish to see the wood factory plantations restricted to already denuded and degraded lands. As the benefits and costs of this issue are analyzed, both those wishing to inflate the benefits as much as possible and those wishing to inflate the costs may be tempted to bring in arguments about the hydrologic/soil/nutrient outflow effects of such conversion. Reliable information on these effects in tropical situations is scarce. In general, however, the greatest effects are due to the conversion process itself rather than to a change in forest. The temporary (one to four years) effects of clearfelling are increased water yield, stormflow, low flow, and on-site erosion (depending mainly on the care with which the products are extracted) and corresponding increased sedimentation, and nutrient outflow. If such clearfelling becomes frequent, and this is usually the case in plantation forestry, these effects will also occur more frequently. Careful harvesting will minimize some of the undesirable effects. If rotations are longer, the effects should be no worse or better than in harvesting native forest by the same methods.

Undesirable increases in on-site erosion and stream sedimentation may be caused by site preparation where cultivation is involved. Contour strip cropping can substantially reduce erosion (and sedimentation) where cultivation must be done, and leaving buffer-filter strips of native vegetation along watercourses can minimize any increase in sedimentation.

There is evidence of little difference, once conversion has occurred, in the variables under consideration between native evergreen broadleaved forests and pine or broadleaved plantations. (The most frequently observed difference is a slight decrease in streamflow.) However, where there is a dormant season characterized by deciduousness in the natural forest, and when it is replaced with an evergreen conifer plantation, there may be substantial reductions in annual streamflow, particularly in the dormant season.

There is really a great lack of information on the effects of conversions in the tropics that considers the wide array of environmental conditions and practices. Studies of low fertility sites in the humid tropics are particularly needed. Second rotations of pines on converted low fertility sites are reportedly suffering declines in productivity, though this phenomenon is not as yet well documented. Nutrient cycling may not be as "tight" under plantation conditions.

Moreover, the current push in the tropics to convert so-called "unproductive" native forest in drier areas to fast-growing species with short rotations (three to eight years) for fuelwood or dendrothermal energy must be accommodated with caution, even though nitrogen-fixing tree species are used in an attempt to solve one of the nutrient depletion problems. Research in this important area is urgently needed.

8
Conversion to Grassland or Savanna for Grazing

Forests may be grazed and the trees cut (often for fuelwood) so that over a period of time (the length of which depends on the intensity of the cutting) the once-forested area is converted to rough grassland for grazing. Burning may be used to hasten the conversion and then used subsequently as a management tool to eliminate successional vegetation and to "green up" the grass. Fodder lopping can accompany grazing in the forest and if overdone can also result in a conversion. Forests also may be clearfelled, the site prepared, and an artificially established (sown) pasture developed for grazing. In many parts of Asia, forestlands that have been degraded by logging followed by unstable shifting cultivation, often may become dominated by coarse grasses such as *Imperata cylindrica.* Burbridge et al. (1981), gleaning information from Indonesian government reports, concluded that "alang-alang" (*Imperata*-dominated grasslands) occupies 16 to 20 million ha of that country, and that it takes over an additional 100,000 to 150,000 ha each year. The Philippines has perhaps 5 million ha of such grasslands (called "cogon") that also include a large component of *Themada triandra* (Sajise 1977). In tropical Africa and Latin America, these degraded forestlands now in grass have other names and other dominant grass species, but the ecological situation is quite similar. Grassland may be the first successional stage in the eventual recovery of a forest, or it may remain as the dominant ground cover in a savanna woodland maintained by grazing and/or fire.

The process of converting forestland to pasture is nowhere more prevalent than in parts of Latin America. The "fiebre del pasto" (the craze or fever to create grazing lands) is resulting in large-scale conversions of tropical forests, especially rainforests. Hecht (1980) describes the conversion process in the Amazon Basin, and suggests that 10 million ha of Amazon forest have been converted, and that perhaps half of these have been degraded and much of them eroded (see Figure 10).

It is therefore difficult to generalize about the hydrologic/soil/nutrient outflow effects of a change in vegetation to grassland, because of these different pathways and somewhat different end products. The type of situation we will consider is usually a grassland characterized by a dense mat of surface vegetation and shallow roots. If the grass is an annual species, periods of rapid growth in the wet season are followed by periods of dying off and no growth. A major problem is that grasslands are grazed, and many

Figure 10. Former tropical forestland in Venezuela, converted to grazing land and showing erosion consequences of overgrazing steeplands.

of them in the tropics are overgrazed. Overgrazing and compaction by animals introduce complicating elements, and when use of fire is added, the comparison of grassland vegetation with forest becomes very complex. Some of the research reported will be grassland conversions without grazing; some will have various intensities of grazing and other special situations, including grazing by different animals. In each case reported herein, the special circumstances will be indicated.

Policymakers are asking whether there are gains in watershed values to be had from preventing further conversion of forests to grass, or from putting trees back on grasslands through accelerated reforestation or afforestation programs. Again, as in other types of uses or conversions, there may be many desirable social, cultural, and economic reasons for converting forests to grassland or vice versa, but here we will deal only with the six hydrologic/soil/nutrient effects already noted. Since most reforestation and afforestation projects take place in grasslands, the effects of that change will be discussed under "Reforestation or Afforestation" in Chapter 12. Here, however, we will be limited to the watershed consequences of converting forest to grassland.

GROUNDWATER, SPRINGS, AND WELLS

Replacement of deep-rooted forests by shallower-rooted grass on deep soils has generally resulted in decreased interception and evapotranspiration losses. One would expect as a consequence greater infiltration into the groundwater system unless the infiltration capacity is reduced by the conversion. While again few good data from the tropics are available, results from existing studies indicate departures from this model as parameters are altered. For instance, where, due to soil conditions, the rooting zone is comparable for forests and grass, or where fertilizer is added to grassland to increase production, water use differences tend to disappear.

Whether or not conversion is accomplished with machinery and soil disturbance (as in an artificial pasture) appears to make a difference in the degree of groundwater recharge. For instance, Boughton (1970) reviewed Australian experience in converting forest to grassland by cutting, burning, and ringbarking (girdling). He found increases in groundwater level when trees were replaced with shallower-rooted native grasses. Boughton has pointed out that where the groundwater was saline, very serious salinity problems have resulted. In one Australian study in Queensland, Melzer (1962) has reported water table rises of 33 feet following conversion to grassland. These increases are apparently most attributable to decreased water use by the replacement vegetation. On the other hand, in Japan, Murai et al. (1975) have found infiltration under *artificially* established grassland to be 20 to 25 percent less than under the forest. They have attributed this to surface compaction due to the large machinery used in conversion and the subsequent trampling by grazing cattle. The Australian studies did not involve mechanical equipment, and the extensive open-range practices result in less trampling than in managed pastures of Japan. Stocking density apparently has an effect.

Other Australian studies in the tropics also suggest that heavy grazing or overgrazing can produce "seals" that restrict entry of water into the soils (Mott et al. 1979). They found that whereas approximately 90 percent of the intensive early season rainfall entered the soil in the grassed areas, only 25 to 30 percent entered the seal areas. Similar results have been reported by Gifford (1978) in Australia's Northern Territory, where the average infiltration rate in groves of eucalypt and acacia was 3.0 cm/hr; between the groves, in grassed areas and areas sealed due to compaction, it averaged 2.2 cm/hr.

On the other hand, in dry southwestern Queensland, Australia, the practice of clearing the trees, windrowing, and burning with heavy machinery (but without sowing grasses) resulted in decreased hydraulic conductivity on clay-textured duplex soils, though not on the sandy-textured duplexes (Cassells 1981, Pers. Comm.).

In Fiji, infiltration rates for grassland were substantially less than under forest, and runoff was almost 100 percent (Cochrane 1969). Runoff coefficients were 0.90 for grass catchments, 0.45 in forest and scrub, and 0.15 in undisturbed forest. This situation may have been aggravated by frequent burning of the grassland. Under these conditions, groundwater accessions under grasslands may decline and compensate in part or entirely for any reduced use of water by grass as opposed to trees.

In Hawaii, Mueller-Dombois (1973) has studied a naturalized introduced grass *(Andropogon virginicus)* that goes into dormancy during the Hawaiian rainy season (October through April). In contrast to closed evergreen rainforests, which utilize most of the soil water that becomes available in the root zone, this grass community failed to remove the water within its root zone. The sites were observed to be swampy, with this excess water condition occurring even into the dry season.

STREAMFLOW QUANTITY

All available research work indicates that there is an increase in water yield when forests are converted to grassland. This occurs not only in the conversion process when the trees are cut, but continues after the grass has become the vegetative cover of the area. Illustrative of this effect is the work by Cochrane (1969) in Fiji. He observed that under normal forest "bankful discharge was not achieved during observations despite heavy rainfall," whereas under grass "a 300-fold increase occurred within two hours from commencement of heavy rain." In converting a tropical forest catchment to pasture in Queensland, Australia, water yield was increased by an average of 293 mm (10.2 percent) during the first two years as a result of reduced transpirational demand (Queensland Department of Forestry 1977).

However, in conversion experiments at Coweeta in the United States, sown pasture given fertilizer and lime and not grazed, showed that streamflow yield increases varied directly with biomass production of grass (Hibbert 1969). When productivity was high, immediately after fertilization, water use by grass equaled that of the forest it replaced. Dry matter production progressively decreased for five years as the fertilizer and lime were used up, and increase in water yield over that of the forested condition rose to 15 cm. When fertilized again during the sixth year, the streamflow returned to that which prevailed when the area was in deciduous broadleaved forest. Grazing would probably lessen this effect, so that with use by animals, even a fertilized grass would yield more water than forests on deep soils.

TIMING AND DISTRIBUTION OF STREAMFLOW

The Coweeta data concerning the effects of conversion to grass (ungrazed) are the most detailed. Hibbert (1969) and Helvey and Douglass (1971) have analyzed the data and reported on this work. Peak flow increased up to 200 percent during the transition period after the forest was cleared and before the grass sod became established. Though water yield increases occurred throughout the nine-year period of the study, there was a shift in timing depending on grass productivity. When productivity was high, grass used more water early in the growing season and less later in the season than the forest. When grass cover was sparser and grass was using less water than hardwoods, the stormflow volume from growing season storms, storm flow duration and base flow rates all increased. Peak flows were not higher once the grass was established.

In Japan, grass and grazed watersheds showed larger direct runoff and peak flows than a forested watershed (Tsukamoto 1981, Pers. Comm.). The nonadapted exotic grass community studied by Mueller-Dombois (1973) in Hawaii gave greater runoff during every month, but especially in the wet season when the grass went into dormancy. An interesting report from some tropical Australian conversion experiments produced results that are somewhat at variance with most other work (Queensland Department of Forestry 1977). A lowland tropical rainforest catchment was two-thirds cleared to convert it to tropical pasture. There was a marked increase in baseflow, but no detectable change in quickflow volume, duration of quickflow, or time to peak. While the annual yield was 10.2 percent greater, the stream was reported to have a more seasonal nature, with dry season streamflow being lower than before clearing.

ON-SITE EROSION

In Hawaii, areas vegetated with non-adapted exotic grass suffer accelerated erosion, particularly soil slips on steeper slopes and channel erosion
on lowland terrain (Mueller-Dombois 1973). This situation has occurred
even in the absence of grazing, though fire has occurred and indeed has
helped to spread the grass. In steeplands prone to soil slips grassland does
not afford the protection given by forests. Steeplands of New Zealand
cleared and converted to pastures have experienced widespread soil slip-
ping, and even though these eroded areas have been treated and revegetated with grass, they have not regained their level of productivity in a
pasture regime compared with uneroded sites (Trustrum 1983).

Aside from this special case, other studies show no significant increase
in on-site erosion between established grass and forest if the grass is not
grazed. In Malaysia, grasslands are not regarded as a major problem in
terms of erosion (Low and Baharudin 1981, Pers. Comm.). In Indonesia,
"alang-alang" covering moderate slopes (approximately 20 percent) under
a 3,200 mm rainfall had a relatively low erosion rate of 3.5 t/ha/yr (Coster
1938). Grassland in one Philippine study had the lowest erosion rate for all
slope conditions of five different land uses, including secondary forest and
forest plantation (see Table 6). In another Philippine study involving swidden cultivation, *Imperata* grassland gave lower erosion losses than all other
land uses except primary forest and softwood tree fallow (see Table 7).

When grazing occurs the situation changes. Considering the propensity
for grasslands to be grazed, and then overgrazed (even with *Imperata*, *Themada*, and related coarse grasses), on-site erosion is always a potential hazard. In the dry area of New South Wales, overgrazing has caused the loss of
up to 10 cm of the surface soil by wind and water erosion (Chorley and
Cowling 1968). The "seals" produced by grazing in tropical Australia
showed five times as much erosion as forest (Gifford 1978). Masrur and
Hanif (1972) demonstrated that in hill land in Pakistan runoff from depleted grass cover was one-and-a-half times that of protected grass cover
(and nine times that of mature chir pine forest), and relative soil losses
under these covers were roughly 80:20:1.

The number of animals seems to be more important in causing erosion,
than the kind of livestock, at least with regard to sheep versus cattle, in the
hill and high country of South Island, New Zealand, (Hughes et al. 1968).
As observed by the author in New Zealand, Hawaii, the southwestern
United States, and elsewhere, even wild animals at sufficient density can
initiate serious erosion in grasslands.

The most serious consequences of on-site erosion occur when the conversion process involves any baring of the soil to establish a sown grassland
or pasture. These increases have been well documented and hardly need
repeating here. Some studies already mentioned in the previous chapter

dealing with site preparation for reforestation would be relevant here. Other work also applicable to grassland and savanna will be cited in the sections on Conversions to Food or Extractive Tree Crops and Conversion to Annual Cropping. Only two specific studies in which conversions to grassland were made will be mentioned here. Murai et al. (1975) in Japan showed increased surface runoff and erosion as a consequence of mechanical site preparation in converting both broadleaved and needleleaved forests to grassland on slopes of 13 degrees to 23 degrees. In the grass conversion studies at Coweeta, United States, the only erosion occurring during the length of the measurement periods was in the establishment phase when the sites were scarified (Douglass 1981, Pers. Comm.).

Tropical Agricultural Hydrology, edited by Lal and Russell (1981), contains several papers reporting on experiments in converting tropical forestland to various other land uses, mostly in Africa. Many of these uses entailed cultivation akin to what would be used in converting to artificial pasture, and may be referred to for specific data.

Burning, which commonly accompanies grassland and grazing, also has effects on erosion. In a study in Amazonian Peru, sheet erosion increased and carried nutrients with it under a burning regime that followed conversion of rainforest (Scott 1974). Unburned grassland minimized such losses.

In Fiji, frequently burned grassland sites with slopes in excess of 20° have active landslips, and 70 percent of the surface shows scars of different ages, whereas under forests, landslips are rare (Cochrane 1969). The increase in landslips on steep slopes reported in Fiji and other places such as southern California (Rice and Foggin 1971) is partly due to the shallower rooting, lower root strength, and smaller root biomass of grasses as compared with trees (O'Loughlin 1981, Pers. Comm.).

SEDIMENT IN STREAMS

Increased erosion from any of the various actions or practices discussed in the previous section may result in increased sediment in streams flowing from the area. Several studies directly measuring sediment have shown this. During conversion to tropical pasture in Queensland, Australia, suspended sediment levels increased twofold during high flows. Levels rose as high as 2,500 ppm during high flows, though there was no change in sediment level during low flows (Queensland Department of Forestry 1977). Even three years after clearing, sediment levels continued to average higher. Cochrane (1969) has reported that while the silt load from forest catchments on Viti Levu, Fiji "was not great," from grassland areas "vast quantities of coarse granite grits were disgorged into Namosi Creek. The turgid, turbid torrents carried great amounts of both fine and coarse materials."

Helvey and Douglass (1971) have reported that in the absence of grazing, once the conversion period was over and grass was established, there was no increase in sedimentation levels over control forest areas at Coweeta.

If there is erosion or potential for erosion, one of the most effective ways of reducing stream sediment increases is through the maintenance of a forest buffer/filter strip along the watercourse.

NUTRIENT OUTFLOW

The most important nutrient losses in converted wild grassland (not cultivated and sown) occur during any burning, or through overgrazing that results in increased surface runoff. Scott's (1974) study of created grassland in montane tropical rainforest showed that burning promoted mineral particle and nutrient losses through sheet erosion. Soil compaction due to heavy grazing and baring of soil due to overutilization both lead to increased nutrient outflow from grassed watersheds because of increased runoff or accelerated erosion. The animals harvest nutrients from the grass. They also move them downslope to water areas as they drink, increasing the rate of export.

In the case of grasslands created by clearfelling, site preparation, and sowing grasses, the conversion process represents a major outflow of nutrients. Cutting the forest alone releases nutrients that move into the watercourses (Likens et al. 1970). Then the method of clearing has various effects. Kang and Lal (1981), though studying conversion to crops of cassava and maize in Nigeria, have shown the effects of site preparation that are also applicable to the present discussion. Their results are presented in absolute quantities in a table in Chapter 10, but are summarized here. Compared to low nutrient losses during manual clearing and no tillage, mechanical clearing resulted in much higher amounts of plant nutrients being removed. The tree pusher clearing method caused greater nutrient loss than the bulldozer sheerblade method.

Fertilization, and particularly overfertilization beyond crop needs for some elements, can result in increased nutrient outflow from managed grasslands. Grasslands containing legumes may increase the total nitrogen content of the watersheds, thus leading to higher nitrogen content of drainage water.

SUMMARY AND IMPLICATIONS

Once forestland has been converted to grassland, the general research experience has been that there is decreased water use, higher water tables, more surface runoff, greater water yield per year, and increased streamflow throughout the year (higher stormflow and higher low season flow).

This appears to be true irrespective of grazing by livestock at least up to a level of severe overgrazing and site deterioration. The picture also may be altered if during the conversion process mechanical clearing has resulted in serious compaction and erosion, especially if there has been gullying. In such cases, there may not be an increase in groundwater levels because of reduced infiltration, which could mean less groundwater accession.

While light grazing in conformance with grassland carrying capacity does not increase on-site erosion, most tropical grasslands are probably overgrazed, and this causes erosion, including landslips, slumps, and stream sedimentation. Stream sediment increases occur especially if riparian strips are converted to grass and grazed. Concentration of stock in or adjacent to watercourses commonly leads to creation of continuous sediment-producing areas through more frequent stream channel erosion. *Imperata* and other rough grasses, which may not be grazed because of low palatability to certain kinds of livestock, may be hydrologically very satisfactory ground covers, with greater water yield than forest and no erosion. Stormflows are increased, and this may not be desirable; low flows are increased and this may be desirable. However, as pressures on land increase, more and more of this is being burned and the new growth grazed, generally resulting in adverse hydrological responses.

Nutrient outflow from converted watersheds increases greatly if conversion is sudden rather than gradual. Clearfelling and site preparation, particularly using large mechanical equipment, accelerates nutrient output. Once grassland is established, the area still may yield greater nutrient losses due primarily to any burning that may be used or due to accelerated runoff and erosion from overstocking.

The major suggestions for watershed land-use policies that arise from what we do know about conversion of forest to grassland include:

1. Minimize soil erosion in any clearing and site preparation activity. Where possible avoid the use of large machinery and control its method of operation where it must be used.
2. Leave buffer strips of forest along watercourses to trap or filter soil and nutrients and to minimize stream-bank erosion.
3. Control the number of livestock, seasonally as well as absolutely, to maintain the sustainable productivity of the grassland and to maintain as complete a vegetative cover as possible.
4. Use the full array of sound range or pasture management techniques (fertilization, moving stock, etc.) that are well-known to range scientists.
5. Refrain from introducing nonadapted grasses that have undesirable water-use characteristics.
6. Control fire frequency and timing, so that fire performs its useful

role of maintaining the grassland against woody plant invasion without causing such undesirable consequences as nutrient loss and increased runoff.

7. Recognize that in many areas of the tropics, uncontrolled fuelwood harvesting, fodder lopping, and forest grazing are converting large areas of forestland into de facto grassland. The watershed consequences of this conversion should be assessed in making land-use policies for control or laissez-faire.

8. Remember that on steep slopes prone to landslips and other mass movements, conversions to grassland usually produce a situation of higher hazard, even without grazing, than the same area in forest; with grazing the hazard is increased by a quantum leap.

9
Conversion to Food or Extractive Tree Crops

The natural forest grows many trees that provide human food and useful extractives, as well as a host of other minor forest products. Use of these has been discussed to some extent in Chapter 1, and the impacts of such use on the hydrologic soil and nutrient variables under consideration in this book have been discussed. The array of food from the forests of the tropics alone is astounding, and was the subject of an entire Discussion Area and Agenda Item (No. 9) at the 1978 Eighth World Forestry Congress in Jakarta. Many other trees provide oils, resins, latex, and saps that can be extracted from the standing tree by tapping. Some of these useful food or extractive species lend themselves to tree farming in plantations. Where they are adapted to degraded lands, rocky places, and rain deficient areas, they may offer economical, sustainable annual crops for such sites, thereby providing food, income, and sound land use. Even on good sites, they may offer an attractive and sustainable substitute for forest production.

The most notable food and extractive tree crops grown in tropical plantations (usually pure, but sometimes mixed) include tea, coffee, oil palm, rubber, cocoa, coconut, banana, macadamia nut, cashew, papaya, quinine, citrus, clove, date palm, durian, fig, Brazil nut, and many others. Where plantations of such trees, hereinafter referred to as "food tree crops" for convenience, have proved to be commercially very attractive, it has led to the clearing of forests and their conversion to these plantation crops. This activity has often taken the form of large "estate" plantations (e.g., oil palm and rubber in Malaysia), though food tree crops can be grown on a small scale on small landholdings (e.g., cloves in Indonesia).

The chief differences between conversion to forest tree plantations (Chapter 7) and conversion to food tree crop plantations are in the nature of their architecture, the spacing, ground cover, frequency and techniques of harvesting, and the rotation cycle. The continuum ranges from small tree or shrub species, such as tea or coffee that are picked by hand and sometimes cultivated between rows, to tall tree plantations such as coconut palm that may have a grass or shade-enduring understory annual crop beneath. It ranges from a relatively long-rotation tree such as rubber (perhaps 25 years) to a short-rotation crop such as papaya (perhaps three years).

In view of the variability it is extremely difficult to make generalizations. Moreover, very few of these kinds of food tree crops have been the subject of good watershed studies. Extrapolations from temperate zone studies with orchards are possible but require care. Temperate zone studies have not dealt with *conversion* from forest to food tree crops in order to assess changed watershed effects, though there have been recent studies of the conversion into apple, peach, and pear orchards on extremely steep slopes in mountainous central Taiwan (Lin 1981, Pers. Comm.).

The best work in the tropics comes from long-standing investigations of tea estates in Kenya and Malaysia and of oil palm and rubber in Malaysia and more recent work with coffee in Indonesia. There is undoubtedly good material from Latin America, particularly about coffee and quinine, but it did not come before this Asia/Pacific workshop.

While there are indeed effects coincident with the clearing of forest and establishment of new plantations of food tree crops, these effects are comparable to those discussed under "Commercial Wood Harvesting" (clear-cutting), "Burning Forestland" (if that practice is used), and "Conversion to Forest Tree Plantations." The effects considered will therefore be those largely occurring after the new plantation has become established.

GROUNDWATER, SPRINGS, AND WELLS

No research directly measuring the effects of changing forest cover to food tree crop plantations on groundwater, springs, and well levels came to the attention of the workshop. The best long-term study of conversion effects is undoubtedly one from Kenya that has been reported on by Pereira (1973) and Blackie (1972). Some inferences may be drawn from this study, which lasted over 13 years through the sequence of (1) forest, (2) forest cleared, (3) tea and shade trees planted, (4) developing cover of tea and shade trees, and (5) full canopy of tea and shade. Initially, there was greater throughfall (less interception) and less water use by the newly established tea plantation than by the original forest, but the differences disappeared quickly. Initially, therefore, there may have been some rise in water table (a phenomenon associated with forest removal for whatever purpose), but there was a return to approximately the original status as tree and shrub canopy closed. Figures 11 and 12 show rainfall, water use, and streamflow of a forest control and a tea plantation. Note that in the drier years of 1965–66 and 1966–67 the tea used more water than the forest—an unexpected effect.

It is thought that other food tree plantations would show a similar lack of major change in groundwater unless they are grazed underneath. However, Teoh (1973), working in 23-year-old rubber plantations in Malaysia, found continued high percentages of throughfall (stem flow, 0.17 percent;

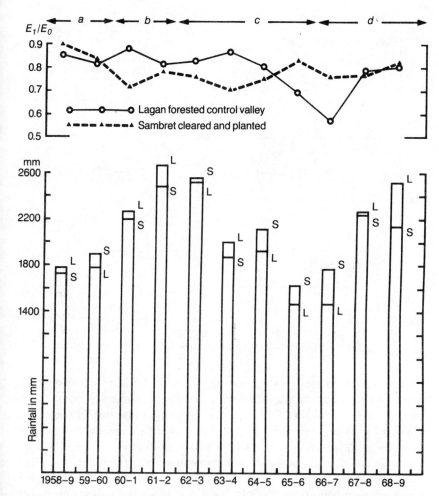

Figure 11. Rainfall and rate of water use, E_t/E_0, of forest (S) and tea plantation (L). The treated valley was (a) under forest, (b) cleared and planted, (c) under a developing cover of tea bushes and shade trees, and (d) under a full canopy of tea and shade.

interception, 24.75 percent; and throughfall, 75.07 percent), which might have contributed to increased accessions of groundwater unless most of it became surface runoff due to reduced infiltration rates from raindrop impact or from grazing, if it occurred.

STREAMFLOW QUANTITY

Conversion to food tree crops results in increased water yield, though this may diminish as food tree crops mature (as in the previously men-

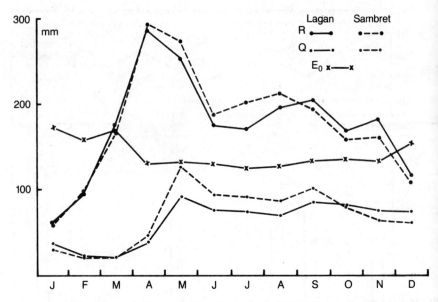

Figure 12. Eleven-year mean monthly values of rainfall (R) and streamflow (Q) for the two catchments—Lagan forested control valley and Sambret cleared and planted—and of Penman EO from the meteorological site.

tioned Kenya tea estate experiments). Much of the increase comes from reduced transpiration coincident with forest removal, and this component may persist in diminished form as the plantation matures. If the tree or shrub crop is a short-rotation crop, however, these increases will occur periodically as a plantation crop with declining product yield is replaced by a new one. Another factor manifest in some food tree crop plantations, however, is increased surface runoff, and this will show as increased yield. In terraced tea plantations, this does not occur. It did not happen even without terracing in the Kenya experiment, in which slopes were about 4 percent (Edwards and Blackie 1981). (See Figure 11 showing rainfall and streamflow by month.) However, Gintings (1981), comparing undisturbed forest with coffee plantations in Sumatra, Indonesia, found substantially greater surface runoff during two different seasons and under different ages of coffee on *steep* slopes (see Tables 15 and 16).

In many Indonesian coffee plantations, even on steep slopes (46 to 66 percent), Manan (1981, Pers. Comm.) has pointed out that every year people come to weed and rake around the trees. This exposes soil, which may then be compacted by raindrop throughfall, resulting in increased surface runoff and erosion.

The effects on the average annual runoff of the process of clearing lowland rainforest (including burning) for conversion to oil palm and rubber

Table 15. Comparison between Undisturbed Natural Forest and a 16-Year-Old Coffee Plantation (*Coffea robusta*) (January – April 1980)

Variable	Undisturbed Natural Forest	16-Year-Old Coffee Plantation
Slope (%)	52–65	46–49
Precipitation (mm)	926.5	926.5
Surface runoff (m³/ha)	104.75	633.37
Percentage of precipitation	11.3	68.4
Erosion (t/ha/6 mo)	0.28	1.18

Source: Adapted from Gintings 1981.

Table 16. Comparison between Undisturbed Natural Forest and Coffee Plantations at Various Ages (May – October 1980)

Variable	Undisturbed Natural Forest	Coffee Plantation 1 year	3 years	16 years
Slope (%)	52–65	59–63	62–66	46–49
Precipitation (mm)	1,338.4	1,338.4	1,338.4	1,338.4
Surface runoff (m³/ha)	101.42	237.94	453.98	837.57
Percentage of precipitation	7.6	17.8	33.0	62.6
Erosion (t/ha/6 mo)	0.31	1.94	1.57	1.27

Source: Adapted from Gintings (1981).

plantations have been shown in three experimental basins in Pahang, Malaysia. Low and Goh (1972) and Toebes and Goh (1975) have found annual increases averaging 10 percent. A recently installed catchment experiment in Pahong is shown in Figure 13.

TIMING OF STREAMFLOW

In the Kenya tea conversions, no significant change in seasonal flows was observed, but according to Edwards and Blackie (1981), process and modelling studies revealed differences in interception and transpiration which in other environments might alter the seasonal distribution of streamflow. However, in Malaysia in two neighboring catchments, one under lowland rainforest (21.8 km²) and the other converted to rubber and oil palm (23.6 km²), it was found that on six occasions when runoff simultaneously exceeded 0.1 m³/km²/sec in both catchments, unit peak discharge values for the converted catchment were between 34 and 140 percent higher (Hunting Technical Services 1971).

ON-SITE EROSION

In Kenya, replacement of rainforest by contour-planted tea estates resulted in no significant increase in erosion (Edwards and Blackie 1981).

Figure 13. Recently installed catchment monitoring in Pahang area of Malaysia to determine hydrologic impacts of conversion of lowland tropical rainforest to oil palm. Forest was cleared in 1981 (photo January 1982).

The investigators point out, however, that similar results would only be obtained under similar conditions: deep, porous, stone-free soils, well-distributed rainfall (more than 2,000 mm, but with a mean maximum of 282 mm and a minimum of 93 mm); efficient soil conservation measures; and gentle slopes (4 percent). Other situations have validated their cautionary conclusions. For example, Shallow (1956) has reported substantial erosion under tea in the Cameron Highlands of Malaysia, where slopes are more than 40 percent without terracing. This was not quantified by direct measurement, but was based on observation and measurements of sediment load in streams from three catchments. Soil erosion rates were estimated as 14 $m^3/km^2/yr$ for jungle (forest) and 269 $m^3/km^2/yr$ for tea. In Taiwan, the author has observed improperly constructed and poorly maintained terraces under tea on steep slopes and subject to typhoon rainfall patterns. These showed dramatic erosion that was not apparent under forest. Lin (1981, Pers. Comm.) and the author have observed the same evidence of serious erosion as an effect of conversion to apple, pear, and peach orchards in similar situations in Taiwan. Gintings (1981) has noted increased erosion rates under coffee on steep slopes in Sumatra, Indonesia (refer back to Tables 16 and 16).

In India, in the Ghats Hills, erosion rates under tea as compared to those under natural forests were reported by Chinnamani (1975) as: natural forest, 0.062 t/ha/yr; tea with a 95-percent canopy, up to 0.224 t/ha/yr; with a 65 percent canopy, up to 0.578 t/ha/yr; and with a 15-percent canopy, up to 4.622 t/ha/yr. These rates do not seem serious, at least under the 95- and 65-percent canopy levels.

Much depends on the ground cover under the tree crop, and its use or lack of use. This is well illustrated by the Indonesian coffee plantations where annual weeding and raking on steep slopes has exposed so much soil between trees (Manan 1981, Pers. Comm.). Rubber plantations are often cultivated between rows in the early years, and this practice produces significant erosion on slopes which are not contour worked. On the other hand, Drysdale and Manner (1981, Pers. Comm.) have reported that in Fiji long-rotation coconut plantations maintain continuous tree cover and have a grass ground cover which, unless it is heavily grazed, effectively prevents erosion. Grazing in rubber plantations, which is being promoted in some areas, has a propensity to result in on-site erosion on steep slopes, unless grazing is very well controlled. In the steep Taiwan fruit orchards, use of herbicides to kill ground cover between trees has resulted in erosion losses, as well as adding chemical materials to the water runoff (Lin 1981, Pers. Comm.). More recently, declining prices for fruit are resulting in less expenditure for grass and weed control, and the erosion potential is diminishing. Cultivating the ground under the tree crop to produce annual crops is called agroforestry and will be discussed in Chapter 11. On steep slopes, such practices can result in increased erosion compared with undisturbed forest.

Erosion rates may increase sharply during the time of tree crop replacement with a new crop. If the mature trees are simply cut and new ones planted without much soil disturbance, there may be little or no increase in erosion. If trees are bulldozed and the ground is prepared for a new crop, only careful methods will prevent major increases in erosion on sloping land. The frequency of such disturbance depends on the economic rotation of the crops. Most tree crop rotations last at least ten years. Banana plants are an exception, but while the individual banana plant has an economic life of less than two years, the vegetative natural reproduction method employed does not lead necessarily to serious site disturbance.

Food or extractive tree crops may introduce another major factor not found in natural forests—the need for a fairly dense and continuously used road network for harvesting (e.g., for heavy fruits of oil palm). In steep terrain, unless very carefully laid out with regard to slope and water handling, and unless well maintained, roads can result in much on-site erosion by simply channeling water and increasing its propensity for rill and gully erosion.

SEDIMENT IN STREAMS

In Malaysia, Shallows (1956) measured sediment yields from three watersheds with different land-use combinations, including forest (jungle), tea, and vegetables. His results are presented in Table 17. Slopes in the Cameron Highlands are often over 40 percent, and terracing with tea is unfortunately not common. These results are to be compared with those reported for the 4 percent slopes with terracing in Kenya, where no increases in sediment yield from forests converted to tea were detected (Edwards and Blackie 1981). Shallows' study also showed that for average and below-average flows, the suspended matter in the streams was mainly organic, but as water velocity increased, the amount of mineral soil (including sand) in suspension increased in Sungei Bertam (see Table 17). At 300 cusecs, the stream sediments were between 40 and 60 percent coarse sand, 52 to 31 percent medium sand, and even some fine gravel.

The importance of ground vegetation along watercourses is evident in Fiji, where banana plantations along the banks of the Rewa River produced little or no sediment because of the good ground cover maintained beneath the banana trees (Drysdale and Manner 1981, Pers. Comm.). Where tree crop estates with sparse ground cover occupy land right to the watercourses, as in some oil palm developments in Malaysia, the author has observed creation of sediment-producing riparian areas which are persistent sources.

He has also observed that roads associated with food and extractive tree crops are often the most important causes of sediment. The heavy and somewhat difficult-to-handle fruit of oil palm leads to rather dense road networks. Adverse effects can be minimized by careful design of the network, design of the road itself, and proper maintenance (see summary for this chapter).

NUTRIENT OUTFLOW

Apparently there have been very few experiments that have compared nutrient outflow from tree crop estates with that of forestland. None were presented at the workshop, and further searching has not revealed any in the literature. As stated previously, the conversion process of clearing the forest (particularly if fire is used concomitantly) results in an outflow of nutrients from the site. With perennial tree crops it is likely that the rate of loss will decrease as the crop ages, till it would soon be at or near the level of the forest it replaced. The nutrient budget might indeed have been reduced, but the rate of loss may not be greatly different once the site is fully occupied by plants. For some tree crops in some circumstances, fertilizer may be added, and this changes the situation. In general, on low fertility

Table 17. Characteristics and Sediment Yield from Three Watersheds in the Cameron Highlands

Area Type	Sungei Bertaim	Watershed Sungei Kial	Sungei Telom
Watershed area (km²)	72.52	21.37	77.70
Area in jungle (%)	64.0	70.0	94.0
Area in tea (%)	21.0	11.0	5.0
Area in vegetables (%)	7.0	19.0	1.0
Open area (%)	8.0	—	—
Sediment yield (m³/km²/yr)	104.0	111.0	21.0

Source: Adapted from Shallows (1956).

soils in the tropics, in the absence of artificially applied nutrients, one of the few sustainable intensive alternate uses of forestland is for food and extractive tree crops, because of the ability of such crops to reduce the "leaks" from the nutrient system.

SUMMARY AND IMPLICATIONS

On suitable sites in the tropics, food and extractive tree crops are an attractive land-use alternative to forestlands. One important consideration in making land-use policy with respect to location and extent of such conversions is certainly the watershed hydrology/soil protection trade-offs between the two forms of land use.

For relatively long-rotation tree crops (upwards of 15 years) in certain kinds of environments, with appropriate soil conservation practices and hydrologically sound roading, there appears to be little difference with regard to important changes in the six variables under consideration once the conversion has taken place. Some of the conditions necessary for this to be true appear to be the following:

1. Minimal cultivation and soil exposure during site preparation following clearing.
2. Construction and maintenance of terraces on sloping lands where a sod will not be maintained (e.g., on many tea, coffee, and rubber estates).
3. Retention of buffer strips of natural vegetation along watercourses.
4. Careful roading with regard to water handling characteristics (slope constraints, outsloping, water bars, culverts where appropriate, minimum density of network, establishment and maintenance of grass cover on surface and banks, etc.).
5. Understory management of ground vegetation so as not to develop surface compaction, bare soil, and erosion channels through avoid-

ance or careful use of such practices as grazing, cultivation, herbicide use and burning.

6. Special conservation measures when a mature crop is replaced with a new one.
7. Selection of long-lived trees that will persist more than one rotation where shade or nursery trees are beneficial.

Where such conditions are not in effect, there has been ample evidence that food and extractive tree crop plantations can produce changes in groundwater, increased annual water yield, increased peak flows and stormflow volumes, increased on-site erosion, increased sedimentation, and increased nutrient outflow leading to diminished site productivity.

Countries like Malaysia, which have adopted land suitability classification systems to delineate oil palm-rubber-cocoa development areas, are to be commended. An additional desirable refinement is the actual spelling out of the performance standards that make such areas sustainable and hydrologically/erosionally suitable. Securing continuous adoption of those performance standards is a most difficult task.

10
Conversion to Annual Cropping

The land-use system considered in this chapter is defined as one where cultivation of the soil occurs at least once annually in the process of planting, caring for, and harvesting a plant crop. Only rain-fed systems will be discussed, since the use of irrigation introduces so many confounding variables in soil and water relations. Even without irrigation, the variables are complex when considering the wide variety of crop species, tillage practices, soils, slopes, degrees of mechanization, and use of fertilizers. Agricultural hydrology (including soil, water, and nutrient conservation in agriculture) is a most important research area, and since food production on farms is a major economic endeavor in the tropics, much attention has been given to this subject. Large efforts have gone into research on the hydrologic effects of tropical agriculture and much has been written. It is beyond the scope of this chapter to treat this topic in detail. Nevertheless, for the sake of a more complete picture of forest land-use options, it is desirable to indicate some of the effects of converting forest to cropland on the six selected water, soil, and nutrient parameters. Only general effects can be mentioned in this chapter, and *Tropical Agricultural Hydrology* by Lal and Russell (1981) should be referred to for more specific information on this topic.

For any particular crop grown, and for any given physiographic and climatic situation, one of the most important factors influencing the impact is the extent to which soil and water conservation farming practices have been used. For instance, on tropical steeplands, well-constructed and well-maintained terraces have permitted stable and continuous annual cropping for generations. Where terraces were not employed, the degraded, gullied, and now largely abandoned steeplands are sad testimony to the undesirable consequences of annual cropping without conservation. As in Chapter 4, "Harvesting Commercial Wood," an attempt will be made to separate the effects on converted lands into two categories: those farmed with and without conservation practices.

The other major impact on water, soil, and nutrients occurs during the actual conversion process, as the forest is removed and the land is made ready for crop planting. When an effect is due to conversion and is only temporary in nature it will be specifically identified.

GROUNDWATER, SPRING, AND WELLS

Conventional wisdom and much popular literature suggest that converting the forest to agricultural land (the term "deforestation" is often used) causes lower groundwater levels and unreliable springs and wells. However, no trustworthy studies were found by either the workshop participants or the author that document this. On the other hand, as has been reported in previous chapters, there are data that show higher water tables following forest clearing (Boughton 1970, Melzer 1962), even to the point where in some instances soil salinity problems have developed. This effect apparently is due to the replacement of deep-rooted trees, which are able to use soil moisture at depth, by shallower-rooted annuals with a lower water use. If soil infiltration rates close to that of the forest are maintained through proper tillage, minimal compaction, and control of surface overland flow, this effect is understandable. On the other hand, there is an intuitive feeling (though no good research evidence) that poor land husbandry, resulting in compacted soils, rapid downhill movement of surface water, and many water channels (rills, gullies), would eventually result in a reduced recharge of groundwater, and therefore in a lower water table, and less reliable springs and wells on the area.

STREAMFLOW QUANTITY

Cutting of a forest to convert the land to another use immediately causes increased water yield from the area. This has been pointed out in several other chapters, but particularly in Chapter 4 dealing with logging. Evapotranspiration losses are reduced by this action. The increased yield persists as long as the regrowth is controlled as has been shown at the Coweeta watershed experiments (Hibbert 1967). If land is planted to annual crops, in effect the regrowth is prevented. As Pereira (1973) has pointed out: "Farmlands under arable crops make a direct demand on water resources and seasonally deplete soil-moisture reserves, but these effects are usually less than those of the natural vegetation which they have replaced." While good long-term catchment experiments in the tropics are few, there is a consensus that streamflow quantity is increased when part or all of a catchment is in annual cropping. Russell (1981), in summarizing the role for arable land use in tropical watershed management, stated: "It is possible to increase the outflow of water from a forested catchment by replacing the trees with short season arable crops, particularly in areas with good rains but a pronounced dry season."

A paired-catchment study on steep slopes (30-degree) at Mbeya, Kenya, in which one watershed was approximately 50 percent cultivated in any given season, gave large increases in water yield (Edwards and Blackie

1981). Low and Goh (1972), reporting on catchment research in peninsular Malaysia, showed an annual increase of 10 percent in water yield in a largely cleared catchment over that from three forested catchments.

There is some indication that the water yield increase due to conversion to agriculture is not much affected by whether soil conservation practices are carried out. Boughton (1970), in his overview summary of the literature as a guide to Australian land and water policy, concluded that there was little effect on catchment yield from practices such as contour banks and terraces (though storage ponds had an effect). He went on to state that the practices that appear to be significant in affecting catchment yield are those with a direct effect on evapotranspiration loss (fallow, changed root depth of plants, fertilization, plant spacing). A 1966 evaluation of a large amount of U.S. Department of Agriculture plot and small watershed data, however, did show some effects of standard soil conservation practices on total water yield. Conservation treatments on agricultural land, as opposed to no conservation, in Texas, Indiana, and Nebraska gave reduced yields of from 25 to 40 percent in dry years, with a less consistent effect in wet years (Sharp et al. 1966). If this extra water went into crop production, it would be a good argument for an on-site economic benefit to the soil conservator.

Many data are from small plots rather than from converted catchments, and too few are from the tropics. Extrapolation from small plots to watersheds and then to river basins is not possible, and extrapolation from a temperate zone to the tropics where there may be year-round cropping is dangerous, considering the importance of the evapotranspiration process. Nevertheless, it seems clear that conversion to annual cropping does increase water yield, probably in proportion to the amount of the watershed cleared.

TIMING AND DISTRIBUTION OF STREAMFLOW

Effects on timing and distribution of water after forest has been cut and replaced with shallower-rooted plants and bare soil during cultivation periods has been discussed previously. In general, there are increases in yield throughout the year, but especially during the dry season (see Chapters 8 and 9). On sloping land, there is usually more surface runoff in cropland than in forestland, and this usually reduces time to peak flow. One exception to this was reported from Kenya where no increased surface runoff was detected on the porous-and-stable-volcanic-ash-derived soils of the catchment under 50-percent cultivation, even on 30-degree slopes (Edwards and Blackie 1981). Cropland usually also has greater stormflow volume, higher peaks, and increased storm duration. It is similar in most respects to sparse grassland cover (see Helvey and Douglass' [1971] results on conversion to grassland). The presence or absence of traditional and well-known soil and water conservation practices makes a difference in these responses (Pereira 1973, Russell 1981).

There are data from many plot studies showing both a reduction and delay in surface runoff from cropland receiving such practices as terracing, tillage on the contour, strip cropping, drainage and contour banks, compared with no conservation. Even in small catchments, these practices and others, such as water storage ponds, are effective in reducing stream stormflow peaks and storm volumes. One cannot extrapolate this to the river basin in making a claim for flood prevention, even for a conversion from forest to cropland. As one moves down the watershed to the lower reaches of rivers, effects are soon dwarfed by the morphology of the basin, the geology of the basin, and the nature and direction of the storm. Another set of important factors affecting floods has to do with accelerated runoff from the nonabsorbing surfaces of human structures and roads; the channeling of water by roads, ditches, and drains; and the extent of human alteration of the river channel and flood plain. To the extent that converting forestland to cropland results in more roads (which may be poorly designed and maintained from a hydrologic point of view), then such an agricultural by-product may also increase local flooding and have a substantial impact farther below the catchment.

ON-SITE EROSION

On sloping land, removing the vegetative cover by clearing forest, cultivating the soil in planting or weeding, and taking off the crop in harvesting have resulted in soil erosion by water. Since soil is the medium for crop production, on-site erosion has been a subject of much concern and consequently of much research. A state-of-knowledge publication, *Soil Erosion by Water in the Tropics* (El-Swaify et al. 1982), focuses on erosion and its control in the croplands of the tropics. Since this topic has been relatively well studied, and material is available fairly widely, only a few selected studies and observations are included in this section of this chapter.

The method of clearing the forest to convert it to the first crop has significant effects on erosion rates. Research on land clearing in the tropics has been conducted at the International Institute of Tropical Agriculture in southwestern Nigeria and has been reported on by Couper et al. (1981). They compared the economics and crop production effects of traditional manual clearing versus two methods of mechanical clearing. Lal (1981), working on the same area, reported on the sediment yield in runoff water (Table 18). Highest soil erosion was observed on small catchments mechanically cleared with tree-pusher/root-rake attachments and then conventionally tilled. This high rate of erosion was observed in spite of the graded channel terraces that were constructed to minimize soil erosion. There was

Table 18. Effects of Methods of Deforestation and Tillage Systems on Sediment Concentration, Water Runoff, and Soil Erosion from Maize-Cassava Rotation (Nigeria)

Clearing Treatment	Tillage System	Sediment Density (g/l)	Water Runoff (mm/yr)	Soil Erosion (t/ha/yr)
Traditional clearing	Traditional seeding	0.0	2.6	0.01
Manual clearing	No-tillage	3.4	15.5	0.4
Manual clearing	Conventional tillage	8.6	54.3	4.6
Crawler tractor/shear blade	No-tillage	5.7	85.7	3.8
Crawler tractor/tree-pusher	No-tillage	5.6	153.1	15.4
Crawler tractor/tree-pusher	Conventional tillage	13.0	250.3	19.6

Source: Lal (1981).

Note: Sediment concentration reported here was from a rainstorm monitored on 31 May 1979.

significantly less soil erosion from manually cleared areas than on any of
the mechanically cleared areas, and less also from no-tillage areas than
from conventionally tilled ones. Erosion was less from plots cleared with
shear blade than with tree-pusher/root-rake attachments. Using Couper
et al. (1981) data, Lal concludes:

> Bringing new land under cultivation is still one of the cheapest
> means of increasing food production in the tropics. In spite of the
> adverse environmental consequences, vast areas of tropical forest will
> be developed for food production. Data presented indicate that
> other than the shifting-cultivation treatment, manually cleared plots
> produced less water runoff and soil loss than mechanically cleared
> treatments. However, manual clearing can be inefficient, time con-
> suming, and uneconomical, and because of the labor shortage, man-
> ually cleared plots may not be ready for cultivation in time. Roots and
> stumps are not properly removed and pose hazards to the equipment
> for mechanized operations. Mechanical methods are, therefore, in-
> dispensable for large scale deforestation for agricultural purposes.
> To ensure sustained productivity, it is important to develop appro-
> priate soil management systems that will minimize the adverse ef-
> fects of deforestation by mechanical means.

On some sites, it is possible that erosion rates will be increased no matter
how the forest is removed. The importance of tree root shear strength in
holding soil in place on areas prone to mass movement has been discussed
previously, particularly in Chapter 4. The work of O'Loughlin and his
colleagues in New Zealand is particularly relevant (see, for example,
O'Loughlin 1974). Moreover, in tropical Australia, Gilmour et al. (1980),
point out that under the particular conditions they have studied, removal
of the vegetative cover can have a major impact on erosion and stream
sedimentation. Their forested catchment was showing saturated overland
flow, and while the stable crumb structure of the surface soil, the surface
root system, and forest floor debris helped to resist the erosive action of
the overland flow, once this situation was altered (as in forest clearing), the
underlying soil of inferior structure succumbed to serious erosion.

If the clearing and preparation process results in erosion channels that
are not stabilized, then these gullies will continue to be a factor in soil loss
throughout the new "stable" regime of the annual cropping process. Oth-
erwise, the impact of the conversion activity per se should be temporary,
and a new erosion rate regime will be established for the agricultural system being practiced. This rate will usually but certainly not always be
higher than the rate that prevailed under forest. Some attention has been
paid to so-called "acceptable" erosion rates while still maintaining a pro-

ductive and stable system of cropping. Some well-terraced cropland on steep slopes has been in continuous production for generations in tropical countries without significant erosion. In Indonesia, it was reported that erosion on unterraced slopes was around 5 kg/m²/yr, more than twice that on terraced lands (Gonggrijp 1941). It is worth noting that many of these fine land-use systems are now showing abundant soil slips that are breaking down the terraces, but they are receiving these mass soil movement effects from new roads, often built into these formerly remote, higher-elevation lands as part of the economic development process.

In general, erosion rates on cropland have been increased over those prevailing under the former forest cover, and if no soil conserving measures are installed, erosion can occur to such an extent that the land must be shifted to a less intensive use. Shallow (1956) in the Cameron Highlands of Malaysia studied sediment yields in streams and extrapolated back to give erosion under vegetables as 404 m³/km²/yr while that under comparable forest was 14 m³/km²/yr (a 30-fold increase under cropping). Manan (1981, Pers. Comm.) reported on a study in Waspada, Garut, West Java, on a 30-percent slope, with rainfall per month ranging from 214 to 244 mm. His student, Arsyik, in a master's degree study found land cover and erosion rates in m³/ha/month as follows: plantation forest, 0.00; corn and peanuts, 3.18; potato, 13.00. Brunig et al. (1975) reported that in Sabah on moderate-to-steep slopes natural forest had annual erosion rates of 10–40 t/ha, while annual field crops had over 1000 t/ha. The classic text on soil conservation in the tropics by Hudson (1971) presents relevant information on soil erosion under various cropping practices, as well as methods of minimizing this process. Many quantified examples of soil losses in the tropical parts of Africa, Asia, South America, and Australia and in Central America, the Caribbean Islands, and the Pacific Islands are presented by El-Swaify et al. (1982). It also should be recognized that the erosion associated with poor cropping practices is magnified in the semi-arid areas of the tropics (Pereira 1973).

SEDIMENT IN STREAMS

Conversion of forestland to cropland almost invariably results in increased sediment yield, especially during the process of conversion and usually thereafter. On-site erosion is responsible for some of this, and it can be the major reason for it (El-Swaify et al. 1982). In fact, many estimates of relative erosion rates in different major drainage basins are based on sediment measurements in the streams and rivers, though there are admitted weaknesses in this approach. Unfortunately, sometimes the weaknesses are not mentioned, and average annual suspended sediment loads are interpreted back to erosion rates, using a "sediment delivery ratio." Sediment in streams can also be derived, however, from soil previously eroded but held in temporary storages until some new activity such as conversion to cropping released it into the stream (see Figure 6 in Chapter 4). Conversion to cropland, by eliminating the storages provided by surface debris and topographic depressions characteristic of forest floors, can release this soil into the stream. Elimination of the important natural streamside vegetation in particular results in the release of stored soil erosion material. Moreover, the increased quantity of water produced by converting forest to cropland can increase the rate of stream channel erosion and the ability of the stream to move more suspended sediment. It is no wonder, therefore, that there are abundant data on sediment yields during and after conversion to annual cropping (El-Swaify et al. 1982).

Here again, the presence and kind of on-site soil conservation practice has much to do with the rate of sediment increase over that which prevailed under forestland use. Mitchell and King (1980) in Australia reported that soil conservation practices applied in a catchment reduced sedimentation rates in a reservoir from 617,000 m³/yr to 206,000 m³/yr in the first seven years of the project.

Douglass (1967) in Malaysia reported that sediment concentrations were rarely below 100 mg/l after conversion to rice, whereas in adjacent forest areas on steeper slopes the concentrations at low flows were between 1 and 5 mg/l. He also described qualitatively the situation in northern Queensland, comparing steep headwater areas still in forest with gentler-sloping, lower reaches mainly in livestock and cropping, and stated that there was invariably increased sediment in the latter situation. Concern over sedimentation of a municipal water supply reservoir in Honduras led to a study of sediment production by various kinds of land use in a 270-km² catchment (Castellanos and Thames 1980). Using the Universal Soil Loss Equation and a Hydrologic Model to analyze the data, they found that next to roads and trails, cultivation on hills contributed the greatest amount of sediment per unit area, and forests the least. Many other examples of sediment yield and stream suspended sediment loads and impact on life of reservoirs are presented by El-Swaify et al. (1982) for agricultural land in the tropics.

The rapid sedimentation of and consequent loss of reservoir capacity has focused much worldwide attention and alarm on the consequences of converting forestlands to annual cropping (and other agricultural uses such as grazing). This conversion process is often called "deforestation," though that term is avoided here because it lacks precise definition. (Some writers include commercial clearcutting or even heavy cutting as deforestation.) There is no question but that rates of sediment transport are increased by most alterations or conversions of forest, and also that conversion to annual cropping is a major cause of increased sediment in streams.

With good soil conservation practices installed and maintained, however, it need not be a major cause for concern. On the other hand, the worldwide economic situation, land hunger, land tenure, climate, and the soils of the tropical developing countries in reality should be cause for major concern in this connection. For example, Wadsworth (1978) has pointed out the threat to navigation (also power generation and water supply) in the Panama Canal due to conversion of the watershed forests to cultivation. He stated that such activity had caused sedimentation in Lake Alajuela to depths of 7 m and that part of the 1977 problem in the canal that forced some ships to send part of their cargo across the isthmus by land was attributable to sediment problems. Similarly, the sediment in the lower reaches of major rivers in India, Pakistan, and Bangladesh that aggravate flooding has often been attributed to the conversion to agricultural lands of forest in the Himalayan foothills and lower slopes. While intuitively this seems to be so, it is difficult to substantiate a cause-and-effect relationship. There are many other factors at work, such as flood plain constriction, increased roading in difficult terrain, changes in water regime causing change in sediment deposition patterns, increased stream bank erosion due to loss of riparian vegetation, and increased landslips due to tree cutting or roads. Nevertheless, conversion to annual cropping undoubtedly has increased sediment problems, and this has aggravated flood problems in some areas and reduced the flood storage capacity of reservoirs.

In addition to the linkage with floods, sediment outflow from agricultural land is linked to another important problem. It is not only a physical pollutant itself (impairing several uses society wishes to make of water resources), but it also carries pesticides, nutrients, organic and inorganic matter, pathogens, heavy metals, and other pollutants into water (Mitchell and King 1980). Several of these polluting materials are associated with annual cropping and are not problems under forestland use.

NUTRIENT OUTFLOW

Nutrient outflow rates from land converted to annual cropping will increase over rates prevailing under forested conditions. In some cases, the rates have increased to the extent that the nutrient enrichment of receiving waters has become a problem (accelerated eutrophication). This situation usually has resulted when faulty agricultural practices prevail.

As previously discussed, cutting the temperate forest immediately releases a flush of nutrients (Bormann and Likens 1981, Likens et al. 1970). It is thought that the situation in the humid tropics may be even more dramatic, since so much of the nutrient budget is in the biomass, precipitation is higher, the cycling is so rapid, and the nutrient pathways are so disrupted by forest clearing. Tree roots and mycorrhizae have been important in humid tropical forest nutrient cycling, and when these are gone there is substantial nutrient loss to streamflows (Golley et al. 1978). One of the most thorough and long-standing studies of nutrient cycling in a tropical forest ecosystem has been that conducted at San Carlos de Rio Negro in the Amazon region of Venezuela. Jordan (1980) reported on one aspect of the work that involved cutting and burning the forest on this site of old, highly leached, low-nutrient-status soils, and allowing one plot to revegetate through successional processes while the other was continually cultivated with cassava (manioc) interspersed with pineapple, cashew, and plantain. Nutrient outflows from the 1-ha plots were measured. Large losses in treated plots compared with forest occurred for K, Mg, and $NH_4 - N$. But the continuously cultivated plot (three years), also showed large differences in leaching of P, nitrates, and especially Ca, enough that Jordan warned that continuous cultivation was not possible without major nutrient additions, and that these losses were sufficient to hinder even the recovery of the forest should agriculture cease.

The interest in maintaining soil fertility by minimizing losses of nutrients through leaching and water runoff has led to a substantial number of small plot studies on this topic. Nevertheless, very little tropical research has been conducted on a catchment scale where nutrients in channeled flow from a forest converted to cultivation (Kang and Lal 1981) have been measured. One of the few studies of this type has been carried out in Nigeria on small catchments at the International Institute of Tropical Agriculture. Measurements of nutrient loss were made under different methods of forest clearing and land preparation and subsequent planting to maize and cassava. Kang and Lal (1981) reported that all treatments gave larger nutrient outflows than the uncleared area, and that largest losses occurred using mechanical clearing with tree-pusher blades and root-rakes, and the smallest occurred in no-tillage treatments as opposed to conventional tillage. Their results in terms of nutrients measured in kg/ha for the different treatments are given in Table 19.

SUMMARY AND IMPLICATIONS

Conversion of tropical forestland to annual cropping has been blamed for a number of important, even catastrophic hydrologic and erosional ills. Indeed, it is true that the pressure on land to grow food has resulted in much ill-conceived land clearing and subsequent land mismanagement, especially as forests have been cleared for cash cropping on ever steeper and steerper slopes and thinner soils. On the other hand, there are many fine examples in the tropics of sustained agriculture that have prevailed for many generations, even centuries, where soil, water, and nutrients are husbanded carefully. Examples exist even on steep slopes, where terraced agri-

Table 19. Runoff and Nutrient Loss in Runoff Water for Different Land Clearing and Soil Management Treatments for the Months July, August, and September (Nigeria)

Clearing Treatment	Tillage Systems	Runoff (mm)	NH_4-N	NO_3-N	PO_4-P	K	Ca	Mg (kg/ha)	Na	Cu^{3+}	Fe	Mn	Zn	Total
Manual clearing	No-tillage	5.3	0.03	0.04	tr	1.0	0.4	0.09	1.1	tr	0.2	0.05	0.11	2.8
Manual clearing	Conventional tillage	24.1	0.1	0.23	tr	2.4	1.6	0.41	4.3	tr	0.8	0.07	0.09	9.9
Crawler tractor/shear-blade	No-tillage	31.2	0.4	0.7	0.01	3.7	1.4	0.52	3.3	tr	2.1	0.26	0.17	12.6
Crawler tractor/tree-pusher	No-tillage	66.7	0.6	0.5	0.08	6.7	4.0	1.36	7.0	tr	3.1	0.17	0.18	23.7
Crawler tractor/tree-pusher	Conventional tillage	94.6	0.4	1.7	0.07	10.0	7.9	1.30	15.2	tr	4.3	0.35	0.58	41.9
Traditional clearing	Traditional seeding	12.8	0.1	0.1	tr	1.1	2.1	0.46	1.1	tr	0.1	0.04	0.09	5.3

Source: Kang and Lal (1981).
Note: tr = trace < 0.01.

culture yields annual crops with little or no erosion, and a hydrologic regime is established that is even more socially advantageous than that in the forest that once occupied the area (for example, many parts of West Java in rice terraces and home gardens).

Because so much depends on which sites are converted and on whether the annual cropping is carried out with sufficient investment in soil and water conservation practices, it is difficult to generalize. The environmental rhetoric about floods, droughts, and land degradation following "deforestation" is not helpful. Equally, the political rhetoric about "conquest of the jungle" by opening up new lands that will feed the masses and offer opportunities for colonization has often in fact led to serious impairment of land and water resources. Some of the myths, misinformation, misinterpretation, and misunderstanding will be discussed in Chapter 13, in an attempt to shed some light on this dilemma. Research evidence in the tropics is so site specific, on such a small scale, or so scanty that it is difficult to derive, research-based consequences of conversion to annual cropping for policies for large areas of watershed land. A few general extrapolations are attempted here, however.

Though most popular writing and even some scientific writing indicate the contrary, research available suggests that groundwater levels *increase* following conversion of forest to annual cropping. This is likely to be true, however, only where soil infiltration rates close to that of the original forest are maintained through proper tillage, minimal compaction, and minimizing surface overland flow by water conservation practices. If poor farming reduced groundwater access, more than compensating for the gains from lower evapotranspiration, then the affected water table might indeed manifest in less reliable springs and reduced well levels.

All catchment studies involving partial or total conversion of forest to annual cropping have shown increased yield in annual streamflow. These increases usually occur throughout the year but especially during the dry season. Stormflow volumes from the catchment usually increase and time to peak is reduced. Soil compaction through inappropriate use of machinery can increase surface runoff and add to stormflow. The roads and trails that accompany annual cropping add to stormflows and rapid movement of water into stream channels so that local flash flooding may be increased. Establishment of appropriate water conservation practices (contour cultivation and ridging, terraces, waterways, careful road and trail location, storage ponds) can minimize storm handling problems of local streams.

Increased rates of soil erosion are a usual but not always necessary consequence of converting forestland to annual cropping. Areas prone to mass soil movement must be avoided, since these areas may be stable only because of the presence of the forest. Once established, these slips and slumps cannot be cropped, and unless stabilized (often at great cost), they will continue to erode and produce sediment with its off-site problems. The effectiveness of good soil conservation farming in minimizing on-site erosion has been amply demonstrated, even on slopes of up to 60 percent. Increased amounts of sediment in streams correlate somewhat to any increased rates of on-site erosion from annual cropping and the conversion process. This could be minimized by maintaining uncleared buffer strips along water courses. In addition, the greater streamflow and stormflow will result in more sediment being produced because of the greater ability of the stream to move bed and bank material. Again, the presence of undisturbed forest vegetation along streams will reduce streambank erosion as a source of sediment. Sediment in streams originating from erosion of croplands may also bear with it such things as pesticides, nutrients, pathogens, heavy metals, and organic and inorganic matter associated with agricultural activities. These can interfere with some of the uses society may want to make of the water, and they are therefore pollutants. Such sediment is best kept back on the land where these materials can be degraded safely.

Conversion of tropical forestland to annual cropping results in greater nutrient outflow from the area in watercourses. In tropical rainforests, this may be especially important, since most of the nutrient budget of the site is in the biomass of the forest. When this is cleared, the cycling is broken and there can be reductions of productivity status due to nutrient leaching and outflow. If these cannot be replaced by artificial fertilization, the period of annual cropping may be short indeed, and the operation may resemble much more an unstable form of shifting agriculture.

If areas of sloping watershed forest are considered for conversion to annual cropping, and if the method of clearing and subsequent methods of agriculture involve no soil and water conservation practices, then the evaluator must recognize that there will result a series of erosional and sedimentation ills, and any benefits of increased water yield may be more than offset by local storm flooding and possibly reduced groundwater levels. There are in the tropics far too many examples of ill-advised government colonization schemes and of spontaneous transient clearing for cropping by landless would-be farmers of unsustainable sites. A legacy has been left behind of degraded lands which will only slowly recover to grow commercial (though often species impoverished) forest. These lands have produced, and will produce until stabilized, erosional material which has entered stream and river channels, creating major problems of reduced reservoir storage and aggravated flooding. Adequate biophysical, economic, and social land assessment/classification aimed at preventing such unsustainable land transformation is an urgent need.

11
Conversion to Agroforestry

Agroforestry is one of the older forms of human land-use and may be defined simply as intercropping woody plants with food or forage crops. It may also be defined in a broader and more comprehensive manner as follows (Vergara 1982):

Agroforestry is any sustainable land-use system that maintains or increases total yields by combining food or other annual crops with tree (perennial) crops and/or livestock on the same unit of land, either alternately or at the same time, using management practices that suit the social and cultural characteristics of the local people and the economic and ecological conditions of the area.

An agroforestry system may consist of a spatial arrangement of crops. Common arrangements are:

1. Trees planted at field borders or farm boundaries,
2. Alternate rows of food and tree crops,
3. Alternate strips of food crops and trees (alley cropping or corridor cropping), and
4. Variable mixtures of food crops and trees.

The sequence of planting trees and crops over time represents another aspect of agroforestry systems. It includes:

1. Alternate or cyclical systems (e.g., shifting cultivation, swidden, bush fallow);
2. Partial overlap in time (e.g., "taungya"), with underplanting at the beginning or at the end of the full rotation or both; and
3. Continuous cropping in a fully integrated system (e.g., Javanese home garden, sylvo-pastoral practice).

A general way of looking at agroforestry systems uses an agriculture-forestry continuum. This consists of a series of possible combinations between agriculture and forestry crops ranging from pure agriculture on one end and pure forestry on the other, with various degrees of combinations in between. Closer to the agricultural end, the system places more emphasis on agricultural output and less on forestry. Close to the forestry end, the system puts more emphasis on forestry output than on agriculture.

Though an old land-use system (or systems) indeed, within the past decade agroforestry has come into sharp focus as a recommendable system of land use for environments where sustainable annual cropping or grazing is not possible. Agroforestry is particularly being adopted by foresters and land-use planners as a suitable system for the uplands and steep slopes of watersheds. An International Council for Research on Agroforestry has been established in Nairobi, Kenya, two agroforestry newsletters initiated, one from ICRAF in Nairobi and one from CATIE in Turrialba, Costa Rica, and at least two bibliographies have been issued, one from CATIE in Turrialba and an annotated one from the East-West Center in Honolulu, all since 1978. In spite of all of this activity, there has been little research on the hydrologic/soil conservation effects of this land use compared with forestland use, reflecting the youth of the systematic study of agroforestry. Sanchez (1979), for instance, stated at the consultation of experts on soils research in agroforestry held in Nairobi in 1979 that "there is no direct information on soil fertility and conservation under agroforestry systems in the humid tropics of Latin America." A scanning of over 800 agroforestry references in the two bibliographies previously mentioned confirmed the scarcity of direct research on the hydrologic/soil/nutrient outflow aspects of agroforestry systems. Most literature is still dealing with describing, cataloging, and classifying practices, considering new species for trials, looking at the socioeconomic aspects, and assuming that soil and water conservation will follow. For instance, the most recent major publication on agroforestry, *Agro-Forestry in the African Humid Tropics* (MacDonald 1982), reports on a research workshop but fails to identify any need for study of the effects of agroforestry systems on these watersheds relationships.

The most applicable compilation of material is the proceedings of an expert consultation held at ICRAF on *Soils Research in Agroforestry*. Yet even though this publication contains an excellent summary of Indian experience by Tejwani (1979), a fine overview by Pereira (1979), and the description of Latin American experience by Sanchez (1979) previously referred to, the inevitable conclusion at this consultation was that there were few research results and a dire need to quantify the effect of inter- and relay-cropping systems and inclusion of trees on soil physical properties (Lal 1979).

Much has been said about the positive influences on the physical environment of the use of well-managed agroforestry systems. Given the lack of specific data, most of these statements are derived from analogies between agroforestry and other types of land use for which there exists some information.

Many similarities exist between certain systems or "stages" of agroforestry and the other land uses discussed in previous chapters. Where total land-clearing is part of the conversion process, the effects on the six variables under consideration would be the same, whether for agroforestry or any other use. If a cyclical system similar to stable shifting cultivation is to be included, as is suggested by Vergara (1982) and others, then the effects of this system sequence have been presented in the section on Shifting Agriculture in Chapter 2. The partial time overlap (taungya) system should have effects at different "stages" than are somewhat similar to conversions to annual cropping with soil conservation (Chapter 10), then similar to either food or extractive tree crops (Chapter 9) or forest plantations (Chapter 7). Where a grazing activity is conducted under planted tree crops, the effects will be similar to those discussed in Chapter 5 ("Grazing on Forestland.") Thus, though there is now little direct evidence from studies specific to the topic of the hydrologic influences of agroforestry, much may be inferred for use as working hypotheses through the innovative use of existing knowledge.

In making inferences, it is important not to be seduced by a mystique that has arisen about the widespread applicability of agroforestry and its ability to solve all land-use problems in the tropics (Budowski 1981). Few long-term studies exist, and to be adequate, studies of hydrologic and soil impacts must extend over one rotation, probably 10 to 20 years (Lundgren 1979). Lundgren pointed out that this is necessary because of the different management activities and ecological conditions that all play upon the site during one full cycle, which include "clearing, hoeing, burning, felling, organic matter removal, shade and exposure, nutrient cycling and various degrees of leaching." He also pointed out the need to include the effect of such climatic extremes as the highest rainfall intensity, or the longest dry period over the rotation.

Research specifically on agroforestry impacts is underway at CATIE in Turrialba. Apolo (1979) has established plots to study sylvo-pastoral systems' impacts on runoff and erosion, comparing bare soil, pasture, pasture plus *Erythrina peoppigiana*, pasture plus *Cordia alliodora*, and unmanaged, densely overgrown land. Also at CATIE, Bermudez (1979) has set up experiments (plots) to study various combinations of coffee and *Cordia*. In Indonesia's Central Java, the author has observed study plots established by van Meer of Gadjah Mada University where runoff and sediment yield from well laid-out plots of various combinations of soybeans, peanuts, and grasses under *Pinus merkusii* and *Melaleuca sp.* are being recorded (see Figure 14). In West Java, work is underway at the Institute of Ecology in Bandung, studying the effects of the complex types of dryland agroforestry

Figure 14. Experimental plots to study hydrologic effects of agroforestry land use in Central Java, undertaken by Gadjah Mada University.

gardens on soil, water, and nutrients, but field measurements have still not been obtained over a sufficiently long period.

In view of the absence of specific results comparing forests with agroforestry systems in their effects on water, soil, and nutrient outflow, this chapter will not have sections dealing with the six variables dealt with in each previous chapter. The few results that have been found will be set forth as individual pieces of work, and an attempt will be made at "summary and implications."

SOME EXISTING RESEARCH

McCauley (1982) intensively studied the complex annual crop/food tree/bamboo/dry land garden systems of West Java, Indonesia, set up a taxonomy, and calculated potential erosion according to the Universal Soil Loss Equation. The "forest gardens" (not cultivated and greater than 100 trees/ha) and even the "thin tree garden" (not cultivated but less than 100 trees/ha) gave good protection even when on the steep slopes. Among those that were tilled but still gave good soil erosion protection were the "mixed fruit" and "mixed bamboo" gardens. Seventy-five percent of the gardens studied were on slopes greater than 30 percent. While the computed potential annual soil erosion losses under all systems seem extremely high, McCauley pointed out that the rank orderings were accurate. There seems no doubt that on these steep slopes, the agroforestry systems with a large number of trees, or systems where forest cover is present at least twice as long as other crops, have less erosion potential than those with less tree representation. These seem to be quite stable systems and probably do not differ much from undisturbed forests in terms of runoff, erosion, and sediment production, as observed by Soemarwoto (1982, Pers. Comm.) and the author. Water yield over the year is probably higher. Nutrient outflow probably is greater in some of the systems, because burning is used in the bamboo rotations ("talun" system).

If annual crops are part of the system, and if it is employed on steep slopes, minimum soil disturbance and incorporation of reasonable soil conservation practices are important in order to avoid increases in erosion and stream sediment. This is emphasized by Pereira (1979), who draws on his work in Kenya with the conversions to tea plantations and on a modified taungya system in a conversion of bamboo forests to coniferous plantations to make observations on agroforestry effects. The tea plantations had shade trees and represented small holdings of 1 to 2 ha, so in a sense they were agroforestry systems. The results have already been discussed in Chapter 9 on "Conversion to Food or Extractive Tree Crops." On these gentle slopes (4 percent) and with a full complement of soil conservation practices, the effects of the conversion over 13 years have been minimal. Soil erosion increases were negligible; water yield increased in the early part of the tea establishment but then returned to about the same; and while peak flows were initially four times as high as the forested catchment, they decreased to about twice as high. Pereira attributes the latter effect to accelerated runoff due to roads and drainageways.

Where soil conservation practices are not employed, cultivated cropping under trees can result in serious erosion. Pereira (1982, Pers. Comm.) has described a demonstration of agroforestry at a forest station in Southeast Asia in which maize and pineapple were planted between pine tree rows straight up and down 20-percent slopes. He also has warned that the taungya system, unless carefully done, is erosion prone when landless families are allowed to grow vegetables between young planted trees in return for keeping them weeded for the two or three years before the trees shade out the vegetable crop. Taungya has also been reported to have produced undesirable erosion in Tanzania, but it is suggested that this undesirable aspect can be mitigated by appropriate soil conservation measures (Hofstad 1978). Pereira (1979) has reported on one of the famous East African catchment experiments involving conversion of natural bamboo forest to plantations of pine and cypress. The pines were actually planted along with vegetables and maize by small-scale farmers in a "shamba" (taungya) system. The vegetable/maize/pine mixture continued for three years at which time the pine canopy made agriculture impossible. It was reported that the system successfully avoided both significant soil erosion and major changes in streamflow. Soil losses were estimated at only about 1 t/ha in the third year, decreasing to about 0.1 t/ha when cultivation ceased. He notes that buffer strips of bamboo forest were left along watercourses to trap any erosion that did occur.

SUMMARY AND IMPLICATIONS

Agroforestry is being increasingly suggested by land-use planners for the tropics as a more stable, sustainable, and possibly even a more economical and more socially acceptable alternative to many kinds of unsustainable agriculture. Moreover, converting many conventionally farmed lands or abandoned slash-and-burn areas into agroforestry systems may produce hydrologic and soil protection benefits. Wiersum (1981) sums up the situation, "The protective function of the trees in relation to soil, hydrology and plant protection can be utilized to decrease the hazards of environmental degradation."

Some planners are also advocating *conversion* of forestlands to agroforestry using the rationale that lands thus converted will be producing much needed food resources, and that because trees are still part of the system, there will be no undesirable hydrologic/soil/nutrient loss effects. It is this conversion and its impacts that are the focus of this section, and that raise some policy questions.

Unfortunately, there are extremely few studies of sufficient duration to provide reliable information about these effects, and one should not rely on mystical notions about the presence of some trees in a grazing or cropping system. As Lundgren (1979) has succinctly stated, "It is often mistakenly supposed that any tree crop has the same stabilizing effect on the soil as a natural forest. This is as wrong as to say that a managed field is ecologically equivalent to a savanna."

Agroforestry systems are numerous and complex. Combe and Budowski (1979) recognize 20 different systems. By oversimplifying and using the general classification mentioned at the beginning of this chapter, some summary statements and implications will be attempted.

The effects of cyclical systems are akin to those of stable shifting agriculture, and since both are small landholding systems, the mosaic pattern on a watershed with different time sequences means a dampening of any effects of specific activities such as forest clearing or burning. Some systems do not involve burning; just as the system of slash-and-trash is used instead of slash-and-burn in some shifting agriculture. This further reduces any impacts, especially on nutrient outflow. Thus on a watershed scale, the replacement of forest with a stable, cyclical agroforestry system is likely to have little effect on groundwater levels, streamflow timing and distribution, and sediment in streams. There will probably be a somewhat increased yield of water each year, some increase in on-site erosion (particularly sheet erosion), and greater nutrient outflow than if the watershed were in forest. The discussion under "Shifting Agriculture" is relevant to this agroforestry system.

The systems which resemble taungya involve underplanting of a cultivated crop at the beginning or end of a tree crop rotation. These systems are usually used to establish forest on open land, but in a few cases may be instituted as part of a program to convert natural forest to tree plantations. Such a conversion may have somewhat greater effects than implementing cyclical systems. First, if this practice is used as a conversion from natural forest, it is often part of a governmental or large private program of replacement with tree plantations. The clearing is therefore likely to occur on a much larger percentage of any catchment, or even involve an entire catchment. Second, there will be soil disturbance during site preparation because cropping between the newly planted trees is a feature of the system. The effects of these activities have been discussed in connection with conversion to forest tree plantations or to food and extractive tree crop plantations (Chapters 7 and 9). They can be of some magnitude, which will depend on the topography, soils, precipitation, and the degree of soil conservation that prevails during the bare soil period. Watershed considerations would suggest that incentives or controls be instituted to minimize adverse effects such as increases in erosion and resulting sedimentation in streams. Retention of streamside buffer strips in natural vegetation should be part of the land-use program.

Continuous-cropping agroforestry systems should by their very nature be sustainable. For this to take place, special soil conservation measures need to be implemented. On steep slopes, for instance, terraces may be needed for the annual crops, with trees (food or forest) planted on the bunds or terrace slopes. Some excellent examples of sustainable agroforestry systems that are protecting soil and water resources have been reported. Though carried out on small parcels, these systems may cover an entire catchment or a large percentage of it. Consequently, water yield usually is higher than that of the forest they replaced. Where downhill water movement is controlled by soil conservation, there need not be major increases in peakflows and stormflow volumes, nor decreases in groundwater level or low season flows compared with forest.

Where the continuous system combines grazing with tree crops, the effects will be similar to those discussed under "Grazing on Forestland" (Chapter 5). Here the main considerations determining the magnitude of the impact are whether or not cultivation occurs for pasture seeding and whether or not frequent fertilizer applications are made. Because of the presence of valuable food or wood tree crops, it is not likely that frequent burning will be used, as is often the case with grazing wild forestland. Stable, well-managed sylvo-pastoral systems will have stocking numbers regulated in conformance with carrying capacity, so that accelerated soil erosion and sedimentation should not be consequences once the system is in place. Water yields will probably be greater than when the area was forested, and the increased rates of surface runoff will probably shift peakflows forward, increase peaks somewhat, and increase the volume of stormflow. Groundwater levels may increase somewhat unless too much compaction occurs, and low flows may be somewhat augmented. Again, it is important that grazing not be permitted right up to the stream bank and along its entire length to prevent the development of riparian sediment-producing areas. (Water access can be provided through appropriate fencing.) On the steep slopes where this type of agroforestry is likely to occur, prior surveys should identify critical areas of potential mass soil movement. Such areas should either be retained in forest or have a high tree density in the agroforestry system to minimize the risk of slumps and landslides. Such critical area determination and precautions should of course be a precursor to any conversion of forest to a different land use. This is particularly critical in connection with a grazing system, because on the steep slopes where mass soil movement is a hazard one of the commonest conversions is to grazing use.

12
Reforestation or Afforestation

Reforestation is generally defined as the natural or artificial restocking of an area with forest trees, including measures to obtain natural regeneration, as well as tree planting and seeding. Common usage has tended to restrict the term "reforestation" to the artificial seeding and planting situation. Where the land has not previously or in recent history grown tree crops, the act of tree planting or seeding is known as afforestation. By 1980, some 18 million ha had been planted in the tropics (Evans 1982).

The man-made forests resulting from such activity range from large industrial plantations to the small plots of farmers or villages. This activity is an important component of many agroforestry and social forestry projects at a modest level, and of large energy "farms" or dendrothermal plantations on a grander scale. It is often carried out as a government activity in the interests of rehabilitation of watersheds, and the anticipated benefits involve not only obtaining a productive crop from the area, but reducing erosion and sedimentation of streams and restoring a hydrological "regulation" to the watershed. Unfortunately, in anticipating hydrologic benefits, many planting schemes are initiated with the expressed or implied purposes of "preventing" floods and restoring undependable water supplies.

In dealing with these watershed impacts, this chapter is different from the preceding chapters in that it represents not the use or conversion of forestland, but putting forest on open land. For the sake of convenience, the term "reforestation" will be used unless there is clear evidence that "afforestation," as defined, is the term that should be used. In general, the effects of establishing forest on open land will be the reverse of the effects of removing the forest, and these effects have been discussed in previous chapters, particularly Chapters 8 and 10.

GROUNDWATER, SPRINGS, AND WELLS

Reforestation of open land usually leads to decreased water tables, with effects most pronounced in the dry season. The additional evapotranspiration demand from a developing plantation as its rooting depth increases will reduce the amount of soil moisture available to recharge groundwater (Holmes and Wronski 1982). In some semi-arid environments, this can cause potentially significant springflow and well-level problems. Cassells (1981, Pers. Comm.) reported on a study in southern Australia that showed that for areas under grass, about 10 percent of the annual 632-mm rainfall reached the underground aquifer, but under nearby pine plantations, no recharge at all occurred. In northern Thailand, Chunkao (1981, Pers. Comm.) also reported a decrease in well levels in dry seasons following reforestation. Similar reductions in water table decline following reforestation were reported by O'Loughlin (1981, Pers. Comm.) on pumice soils planted to *Pinus radiata*, by Boughton and Bonell for Australia where there was a strong dry season (1981, Pers. Comm.), and by Douglass (1981, Pers. Comm.) for the coastal plain of southeastern U.S.

While intuitively one might think the increased evapotranspiration loss would be more than compensated for where compacted and degraded lands had their infiltration rate substantially improved by virtue of reforestation, there are no experimental data to support this conclusion. Nevertheless, in many tropical developing countries, citizen support for expanded reforestation programs is being at least partly marshaled by unfounded claims that such programs will restore unreliable springs and raise water levels and yields in wells. No research results are yet available about whether reforestation in fog or cloud areas could add to groundwater resources.

STREAMFLOW QUANTITY

Similarly, in much popular writing and political pronouncements, reforestation or afforestation is being advocated to make more water available in streams for human use. In fog or cloud forest areas, planting trees can increase the effective moisture reaching the ground (Ekern 1964) and might more than compensate for increased water use by the forest. Unfortunately, no stream yield data are available for this situation. In all other cases following reforestation, research results show a *decrease* in total water yield. *Banks and Kromhout* (1963) showed that in the Jonkershoek catchments of South Africa there were decreases in streamflow beginning the fourth year after planting and continuing to about the twelfth year, when it remained relatively constant but at a lower level than prior to reforestation. In these experiments, natural sclerophyll scrub was replaced with *Pinus radiata*. Similar results were obtained in the Transvaal in afforesting grassland with *Eucalyptus grandis* and *Pinus patula* (Van Lill et al. 1980). The eucalypt influence began three years after planting, with a maximum reduction in flow (expressed as rainfall equivalent) of between 300 and 380 mm/year. Decreases from the pine planting were delayed a year and were smaller than that under the eucalypt.

In Fiji, the extensive reforestation and afforestation programs in the "dry zone" grasslands have resulted in reduced water yield in streams, causing considerable concern, and this has sparked a major research endeavor by the Fiji Pine Commission (Manner and Drysdale 1981, Pers. Comm.). At Dehra Dun in India, Mathur et al. (1976) reported yield decreases of 28 percent following afforestation with eucalypts. The long-term and well-known Pine Tree Branch Watershed studies in Tennessee produced convincing evidence of reduced water yield following reforestation, mainly with several pine species (Tennessee Valley Authority 1962). Many other studies from the temperate zone had similar results, so there seems little doubt that soon after reforestation, total water yield in streams from the planted catchments decreases. Bosch and Hewlett (1982) suggested that the decrease is proportional to the growth rate of the stand.

TIMING AND DISTRIBUTION OF STREAMFLOW

The evidence suggests that the decrease in yield discussed here is greatest during the low flow period. It was an apparent 50-percent reduction in minimum flows over the period 1969–1978 and a 65-percent reduction in yield over the low-flow period that initiated the current concern in Fiji (Kammer and Raj 1979; Manner and Drysdale, 1981 Pers. Comm.). A different result has been obtained in Indonesia, however, by Hardjono (1980) in comparing an agricultural watershed with one 25-percent reforested and one entirely reforested (using *Pinus merkusii, Tectona grandis, Swietenia macrophyla,* and *Eucalyptus alba*). He reported continuous streamflow during the dry season from the reforested areas, 2.5 times that of the agricultural watershed. However, there may be additional variables involved, since the study was not done in a completely controlled experimental catchment series.

With respect to stormflows and peakflows, there are some differences in results, though most experiments have shown somewhat smaller stormflow volumes, marked reductions in peakflows, and a marked delay in peaking. The Pine Tree Branch experiments carried out from 1941 to 1960 showed not only a great reduction in highest seasonal peaks, but decreases in peak discharges from comparable preplanting and postestablishment storms over the entire range of moisture conditions, rainfall intensity, and season (Tennessee Valley Authority 1962). For instance, the time required for 20 and 95 percent of the water to discharge from the watershed was increased some 5 and 18 times, respectively, and the reductions in peak discharge ranged from 92 to 97 percent in the growing season and 71 to 92 percent in the dormant season. Tsukamoto (1981, Pers. Comm.) in Japan, reported that peak flows were 1.4 times greater in the denuded watershed than the reforested one. On the other hand, Dragoun and Harrold (1971), in working with an 18 ha catchment *on shallow soil* in

Ohio (U.S.A.), found that pine reforestation produced no effect on either the maximum stormflow peaks or the hydrograph shapes.

Analyzing the long-term South African experiments involving afforestation of periodically burned, natural veldt catchment, Hewlett (1982) reported on work underway with his collaborator, Bosch, and stated that there has been no change over the years in either peakflows or stormflow volumes. These are deep soil catchments with 2,500-mm rainfall per year and normally have small stormflow responses.

In reviewing his experience with research results and the experience of the workshop participants, Megahan (1981, Pers. Comm.) suggested that peaks may increase or decrease depending on the previous vegetation, land use, soils, and rainfall pattern and that it is a complex matter; the most common experience, however, has been for a decrease in stormflow peaks.

One other aspect of timing and distribution has been noted in Fiji, where following tree planting more pronounced diurnal fluctuations were noticed, especially in the dry season, when there occurred 40-percent differences between maximum midmorning flows and minimum early evening flows (Kammer and Raj 1979).

ON-SITE EROSION

A major reason for undertaking reforestation or afforestation is to reduce erosion rates that prevail under some existing nonforest land use. Both practical and research experience have shown that once forest tree plantations have been established on formerly open land, erosion rates show significant reductions. Most research studies actually have measured stream sediment yield from an area and suggested that this indicates the extent of erosion due to some treatment. The shortcomings to this inference have been discussed previously. Nevertheless, there is some validity in the suggestion that sediment yield rates are *indicative* of erosion rates. Moreover, sediment yield from the catchment does integrate soil movement from the various activities associated with the land-use treatment. For instance, associated with reforestation there may be cultivated fire lines and roads for access that are susceptible to erosion but would not be included were one to simply measure on-site erosion in the plantation.

There is no question but that gullies have been stabilized and sheet erosion dramatically reduced by reforestation, once a leaf litter has become established. Grass cover also is undeniably effective in minimizing erosion, but where there is grass, there is grazing (and often fire), and erosion rates are therefore usually higher than under forest plantations. Reestablishment of trees can again provide root shear strength to minimize shallow soil slips on areas prone to mass movement following storm events (O'Loughlin 1981, Pers. Comm.).

Eroded soil depth over time following reforestation of a denuded slope in Japan was shown by Tsukamoto (1981, Pers. Comm.) to decrease as follows: 0.71 mm in the first year, 0.50 mm in the fifth year, 0.34 mm in the tenth year, and 0.05 mm in the fifteenth year for the whole watershed. He also reported a rate reduction from 72.36 m³/ha/yr to 0.17 m³/ha/yr as seven-year averages on adjacent slopes, one denuded and one reforested to pines. Hardjono (1980) in Indonesia showed decreasing soil losses in sub-watersheds as the percentage of reforested area increased from totally agricultural to 100 percent reforested. Manan and Drysdale (1981, Pers. Comm.) reported similar trends in erosion rate reductions in Fiji in the Lakeba catchment.

The general consensus about decreased erosion regimes following reforestation does not mean that the erosion problem vanishes. There can be significant erosion under forest plantation cover in steep slopes depending on the nature of the understory vegetation (or lack of it) and the characteristics of the litter and forest floor in general. Reference has already been made in Chapter 7 concerning certain problems reported in teak plantations (Bell 1973, Kunkle 1978, Michaelson 1975). Brunig et al. (1975) reported annual erosion rates in tons per hectare on moderate slopes for undisturbed natural forest, teak plantation widely spaced with mixed understory, and dense teak plantation with no understory, as 0.2 – 10, 2 – 10, and 20 – 160, respectively. Perino (1981, Pers. Comm.) indicated that in the Philippines there appeared to be greater erosion in reforested areas under *Alnus maritime* than under *Pinus kesiya*.

Moreover, one reason for the reduced rates of erosion that characterize reforested lands is that this generally leads to a much less intensive use of the area by man and animals. In very short-rotation energy plantations of fast-growing trees, especially under mechanical harvesting, some of this comparative advantage evaporates. The section on On-Site Erosion in Chapter 4 discusses erosion problems associated with forest harvesting, and Appendix C deals with guidelines for minimizing erosion impacts of this activity. Care in harvesting is especially needed for short-rotation plantations.

An additional erosion problem situation arises in connection with any soil disturbance associated with preparing the site for planting and with subsequent cultivation to reduce competition in the early establishment phase. Ball (1981) suggested that clearing and cultivation were necessary in Nigeria for establishing forest plantations. A comprehensive set of monitored catchment studies involving exotic pine reforestation under various methods of site preparation have been carried out in Queensland, Australia, since 1974. The initial results have been published by Cassells et al. (1982). They indicated that, "since the first plantings in 1974, the initial establishment phase has been accompanied by significant erosion and stream sedimentation." "Broadcast ploughed areas" showed the greatest erosion and "no cultivation" showed the least (but the latter also showed the least satisfactory plantation development). The authors reported that contour strip ploughing has now been adopted as routine practice on erodible soils. A set of planting site preparation guidelines for Queensland is currently being promulgated (Cassells 1982, Pers. Comm.). In Fiji, the pine planting program of the Fiji Pine Commission in the dry zone does not involve cultivation but does include roading, and Drysdale (1981, Pers. Comm.) indicates that until recently these were not engineered to a high enough standard to prevent serious erosion from surfaces and banks in the wet season. He indicated also that some erosion occurs during the pre-planting burning of the grassland. The Fiji Pine Commission also is developing some energy plantations with eucalyptus species in the dry zone, and Bell and Evo (1982) pointed out the need for full cultivation prior to and during the first year of establishment with eucalypts, and they state that this also has been the general experience elsewhere. If reforestation in the tropics does require intensive site disturbance to achieve satisfactory establishment and growth, soil conservation measures from agriculture will be needed to avoid accelerating erosion during the one to three years before a new protective baseline is achieved by the new forest.

SEDIMENT IN STREAMS

Greatly reduced sediment yields are usually achieved from reforestation or afforestation. Once established, reductions from previous land uses have been well documented. Hardjono (1980) for instance, reported the results from subwatsheds in Indonesia that are given in Table 20. The reforested areas were planted with *Pinus merkusii, Tectona grandis, Swietenia macrophyla,* and *Eucalyptus alba.*

One of the classic studies of the impact of reforestation on stream sediment was conducted from 1941 to 1960 in Tennessee, (U.S.A.), on a 36-ha watershed that had at one time been almost 100 percent in cotton and maize. At the time of study initiation it was reported that half the area was idle and severely eroded, less than one-quarter was in poor forest, and the remainder was in row-crop cultivation or eroding pasture (Tennessee Valley Authority 1962). Following total reforestation, mainly with *Pinus taeda,* plus some check dams and grassing of gullies the average reduction in total sediment from 10 to 15 years after treatment was 96 percent. Sediment dropped from around 58 t/ha/yr to 3 t/ha/yr, though there was a marked decrease in mean annual precipitation from the first period to the last.

Temporary substantial sediment increases can occur above that of some previous land uses due to new roading and site preparation work. The recent Queensland study by Cassells et al. (1982) presented excellent data

Table 20. Average Annual Soil and Water Effects of Reforestation Compared
with Agricultural Use in Central Java

Variable	Upland Dry Agriculture	Land Use 25% Reforested	100% Reforested
Watershed area (ha)	207	163	354
Slope (%)	28	28	43
Precipitation (mm/yr)	2,444	2,070	2,618
Discharge (m³/sec)	38.31	23.30	48.83
Unit discharge (m³/sec/ha)	0.175	0.155	0.137
Suspended load (t)	4,171.84	2,215.18	2,880.45
Sediment yield (t/ha/yr)	20.15	13.59	8.14

Source: Hardjono (1980).

on sediment effects of various kinds of plantation establishment methods under different soil and previous land-use situations. This study particularly highlighted the role of buffer strips along watercourses. Such areas should not be cultivated in the planting process but should be hand planted. They reported that in the absence of buffer strips, there were not only dramatic increases in sediment concentrations for the first two years, but that streambank sediment sources created by site preparation continued to yield accelerated levels of sediment well into the rotation. Roads and firebreaks must be laid out carefully and well maintained if they are not to be sediment-producing features. Appendix C suggests some guidelines for ameliorating this impact from these sources.

NUTRIENT OUTFLOW

Nutrient outflows from reforested catchments, or even plots, compared with those from agricultural cropland or grassland, have not been researched extensively. It is thought that nutrient outflows would be reduced, particularly if fertilizers had been part of the previous land-use system, or where there had been active erosion that found its way into watercourses as sediments. The use of nitrogen-fixing trees in reforestation might alter the situation. Short-rotation tree harvesting would likely speed up the outflow of nutrients compared with long-rotation trees, unless it were a coppicing system or seedling regeneration immediately obtained by natural or artificial means.

SUMMARY AND IMPLICATIONS

In tropical countries, there is a widespread popular belief that reforestation will improve groundwater aquifers and result in not only more water in streams, but in "more reliable" flows, i.e., greater low flows. Such a belief is partly responsible for the support of watershed tree planting programs in the Philippines (Saplaco and Perino 1981, Pers. Comm.), in Thailand (Chunkao 1981, Pers. Comm.), in Indonesia (Manan 1981, Pers. Comm.), in Malaysia (Low 1981, Pers. Comm.), and in Papua New Guinea (Vergara 1981, Pers. Comm.). It is only within the past two years that it has been questioned in Fiji (Manner and Drysdale 1981, Pers. Comm.), at least in government circles. This belief is not unique to laymen in tropical countries, for it pervades much of the popular writing in the temperate countries also. Yet the overwhelming evidence from catchment research is that following reforestation, groundwater levels are lowered and stream yields are reduced, both effects being more pronounced in the dry season or growing season. A possible exception exists when reforestation occurs in areas of potential fog or cloud water capture, but there are as yet no field experiments that show this conclusively.

There appears to be enough evidence to indicate a benefit in some situations in affecting stormflow patterns to reduce the severity of *local* flooding. Storm peakflows are usually reduced and delayed. Stormflow volumes may or may not be reduced, depending on the prereforestation land use. Any effect on reducing local flood severity, however, cannot be extrapolated to large river basins in a claim for flood prevention benefits. The effect of vegetation changes is rather quickly overwhelmed by other river basin variables. Countries that have instituted large reforestation or afforestation programs in order to *prevent* floods on major rivers (e.g., Yangtze, Indus, Ganges, Mekong) will not eliminate floods by this program alone. There are, however, many other good reasons for large watershed reforestation programs.

One very real benefit from reforestation is to reduce the erosion rates that prevail under most other land-use systems. To obtain maximum benefit, however, it is necessary to direct soil and water conservation efforts to any roading, site preparation, and early soil cultivation work necessary in the establishment phase and to the site disturbance occasioned by the ultimate harvesting. For fast-growing, short-rotation plantations desired for fuelwood and energy plantations, the harvesting disturbance produces accelerated erosional situations frequently enough that some of the soil protection benefits, which are functions of less intensive human and animal use, are lost. Trees that coppice for at least a few rotations can eliminate some of the need for repeated site preparation and cultivation. Instituting certain practices during harvesting can minimize erosion (see Guidelines in Appendix C).

Watershed rehabilitation through reforestation or afforestation can indeed cause major reductions in stream sediment loads. In this respect, it is particularly important to stabilize landslips or landslip-prone areas with forest trees. It is important also to establish undisturbed riparian buffer strips by reforestation and to refrain from cultivation during the establishment. Roads and firebreaks can be important, persistent, sediment-producing areas and should be designed and maintained with due attention to soil and water impacts (see Appendix C and Megahan 1977).

It also appears that any nutrient levels in streams that cause problems to stream users or represent serious losses to the site in question may be reduced through establishing plantation forests on open land.

In summary, it is appropriate to quote Sir Charles Pereira (1973) who quite aptly stated: "Surveying this scattered experience, it is clear that forest should neither be felled nor planted on a large scale without a study of the potential hydrological changes which may be expected."

13
Rethinking Some Watershed Policies*

In many developing countries, land-use policies for forestlands are being suggested on the basis of the forest's assumed roles in influencing certain hydrologic, soil-erosion-protection, and sedimentation-minimization characteristics of watersheds. In some cases, these roles have been proven scientifically; in some cases they are folklore or myth—or misinterpretation of research. Whatever the case, it seems desirable to conclude by shedding some light on a few of the four Ms (myth, misinterpretation, misinformation, and misunderstanding) about the effects of using or converting tropical forestlands, in a watershed land-use context.

For instance, it is suggested that cutting of rainforest will result in desertification. There is no evidence that rainfall on the area will decrease to the point where the area becomes arid. It also is suggested that reforestation or afforestation of open lands, including extensive grasslands, will cause well levels to rise, springs to flow again, and low flows in streams to increase. All evidence from temperate zone research, however, indicates the reverse. Is this research inapplicable to the tropics or are we using the wrong arguments for the right reasons? Floods in the lower stretches of major rivers, such as the floods in Bangkok and New Delhi, are blamed on tree harvesting or shifting cultivators in the uplands far away. This relationship has never been proved, but could it still be correct and therefore a basis for land-use policies? Or are urban people refusing to look at their actions in flood plain occupancy, channel constriction and alteration, and the effects of such important sediment-producers as roads?

Some of the policies discussed in this chapter have been promulgated or advocated with claims of a sound rationale of soil or water conservation, but which in fact have no scientific basis, or worse, have a countervailing scientific basis.

---

*This chapter presents some of the author's thoughts, which are not necessarily endorsed by the participants of the watershed workshop that initiated this publication.

CUTTING FORESTS REDUCES RAINFALL?

It is being advocated that we save tropical forests, particularly tropical rainforests, because cutting them will convert the areas into deserts and create droughts. The World Wildlife Fund/IUCN Tropical Forests Campaign was initiated in October 1982 at Bali in Indonesia. It suggested that following logging, the "land of green gold" is turned into "useless desert" and that "take away the trees and you get withering drought in the dry season" (WWF/IUCN 1982). Suggestive of the same thinking was the title of an influential book, *Amazon Jungle: Green Hell to Red Desert?* (Goodland and Irwin 1975). The leader of the Tree Hugging Movement (Chipko) in India has claimed that cutting of the forest results in droughts (Anonymous 1981). In an article entitled, "The Desertification of Asia," it is claimed that "deserts can develop with great speed even in the heart of a tropical jungle" (Sharp and Sharp 1982). In these cases, there may be some slippery semantics in the words "desert" and "drought," but a dictionary suggests that a desert is "arid land with insufficient precipitation to permit plant growth," and that a drought is "lack of precipitation or moisture." It is hard to see how a tropical moist forest area receiving upwards of 1,800 mm/yr of rain can be converted into a desert by logging.

Early forest influence research, showing little or no relationship between presence or absence of trees and the precipitation falling on that area, was synthesized and brought into the policy arena in the tropics by Pereira in 1973 (Pereira, 1973). Yet the idea persists that local rainfall is reduced by cutting forests, and the author has encountered folklore to this effect, particularly among banana growers in Central America and policymakers in South Asia. It is true that there is some recent work in the Amazon Basin suggesting that for this large area with its unique hydrometeorology, the forest does regenerate some of its own rain (Salati et al. 1979) and that possibly, therefore, *large-scale* and *permanent* deforestation (not just logging) could reduce or alter rainfall in parts of it (Salati 1981). This speculation has not yet received a ringing scientific endorsement.

Saving fine examples of complex tropical lowland rainforests from the logger is indeed a worthy cause. Indeed, there are many compelling, scientifically sound, and philosophically rewarding reasons for trying to preserve a large amount of the world's remaining primary tropical rainforest, but fear of reduced rainfall is not one of them.

One exception to that rule occurs, however, in certain physiographic situations. For example, in coastal fog belts or at high elevations characterized by frequent or persistent cloud, forests can "capture" and condense atmospheric moisture. This so-called "occult" precipitation is added to the effective moisture received by the area and may represent a substantial percentage of the total. For example, in Hawaii it represented an extra 760 mm above a nonforested 2,600 mm of rainfall (Ekern 1964). Cutting down the forest results in loss of this occult precipitation, though it is restored as the forest regrows. If the area is converted to another use, this moisture is removed from the water budget of the watershed, including water outflow from the immediate watershed (Zadroga 1981). Therefore, saving cloud forests and fog forests makes good hydrologic sense.

CUTTING OF FORESTS DRIES UP WATER SUPPLIES?

There is a widespread belief that logging of tropical forest watersheds has caused wells, springs, streams, and even major rivers to cease flowing, at least during the dry season (Eckholm 1976, Sharp and Sharp 1982). Policies to set up protection forests that may not be cut are being advocated because of a supposed "sponge" effect that soaks up water in the wet periods and lets it release slowly and evenly in the dry season to keep water supplies adequately restored. It is difficult to reconcile such policy with small watershed cutting experiments that almost universally have given *increased* total water yields over the year, with the greatest increases usually in the low-flow months. Bosch and Hewlett (1982) have reviewed 94 controlled-catchment studies and reinforced this relationship. They have even indicated some predictive quantification as to the amount of increase. Moreover, most cutting experiments have shown increases in groundwater levels (Boughton 1970).

Perhaps some of the dilemma arises because of semantic problems. The catchment experiments involved forest cutting and logging, *not* conversion to another use such as grazing or annual cropping. The real-life problem in the tropics is that forest harvesting is often the precurser to a conversion, and the term "deforestation" (which is often used) may refer to the sequence of logging, clearing, and then unsustained agriculture or grazing without soil and water conservation. If compacted surfaces with intervening and frequent gullies are the end result (and one finds such landscapes all too commonly in the upland tropics), then it is possible that there may result such things as lower water tables (less reliable springs and wells) and lower dry-season flows in streams. There are no large-scale, long-term experiments to support this intuition and professional judgment. Correlations of land area deforested over time and decreased streamflows are not cause and effect, though such a relationship has often been claimed by writers using such statistics.

One problem is that most controlled watershed experiments are in the temperate zone. The few reliable tropical paired-catchment experiments that do exist, however, do not indicate any different results.

In some instances, there are valid reasons for establishing totally protected watershed forests with no forest harvesting permitted, but concern that cutting will result in dried up wells and springs and ephemeral streams where perennial streams once prevailed does not have a scientific basis. Conversion and subsequent land degradation on a large scale may be a different story.

CUTTING OF FORESTS CAUSES FLOODS?

There is indeed an intuitive feeling (based, however, on some scientific evidence) that forest cover on a watershed does offer the best guarantee against local flash flooding. However, one must become somewhat uneasy when hearing statements that "forests guard against flooding" (European Environmental Bureau 1982) because the persons saying this are referring to major floods on large rivers. Belief in this statement about the hydrologic safety of forest cover gets misinterpreted to mean that if forests are cut, major floods will be the consequence. Thus, monsoon floods in the Ganges and the Indus (which have always occurred) have been attributed to tree cutting in the uplands (World Water 1981). A statement by Openshaw (1974) that "the principal cause of the recent floods in the Indian subcontinent was the removal of tree cover in the catchment areas for fuelwood," was recently repeated at the 1978 World Forestry Congress (Avery 1978). In the Philippines following the great Agusan flood of 1981, the state minister placed "30 percent of the blame on logging" of headwater forests, even though "flooding is an annual event, and major floods are expected about every 20 years" (Corvera 1981). There followed in the same newspaper an interview with a top official in the Philippine Bureau of Forest Development on the subject of actions by that organization to control logging and encourage reforestation. It has been suggested that "overlogging is now officially recognized as the cause of last July's severe flooding of the Yangtze" in China (Sharp and Sharp 1982).

Are these popular concerns about forest cutting and floods valid, or are they misinterpretations of research findings? Are people looking for a scapegoat so that they do not have to consider that floods have always occurred, but that damage is truly increasing because of greater flood plain occupancy, greater channel constriction, and alteration by human structures?

Findings from paired-catchment research in which one catchment has been logged indeed usually (but not always) show greater stormflow volumes, higher peakflows, and earlier peaks in streams emanating from the logged area (Douglass and Swank 1975, Reinhart et al. 1963). Flooding may be increased close to the area cut, but as water is routed down a major river basin, this effect is rather quickly reduced to insignificance amid other processes of paramount importance, such as the nature and intensity of the precipitation, the direction it moves across the basin, and the size and morphometry of the basin. Hewlett (1982) has recently examined the evidence worldwide from forest watershed research and reported that there was no cause-effect relationship between forest cutting in the head-waters and floods in the lower basin. Even if a whole basin were under a forest harvesting regime, normally it would not be logged off all in one year. Those portions that are logged rather quickly return to a prelogging hydrologic regime as the forest regenerates and full canopy is restored, even though it is young growth. Moreover, a substantial part of this stormflow/peakflow effect is due to poorly located and designed roads, skid trails, and log landings, all of which speed water off-site. Thus, proper conservation logging can reduce any small effects on upstream flooding. Floods occur due to too much precipitation falling in too short a time or over too long a time (prolonged), beyond the capacity of the soil mantle to store it and the stream channel to handle it.

The previous discussion has referred to the impacts of forest harvesting on floods, not on the effects of forest harvesting followed by conversion to agriculture and grazing and subsequent degradation by misuse. Such de-graded areas, encompassing whole river basins, may indeed aggravate flooding and be one of the principal causes of serious flood damage. How-ever, if converted to controlled grazing lands or agriculture under a sound soil and water conservation regime, such watershed land use should no more *cause* floods than would careful forest harvesting.

SHIFTING AGRICULTURE IS RESPONSIBLE FOR MASSIVE EROSION AND ACCELERATED RESERVOIR SEDIMENTATION?

In the press, in environmentalist writings, in political pronouncements, and even in some literature from land-use professionals, shifting agricul-ture has been condemned as causing many of the environmental ills in the tropics (European Environmental Bureau 1982).

Aside from eliminating primary tropical forest (an inevitable conse-quence of shifting agriculture that does have serious policy implications) this ancient land-use system is most specifically targeted as causing mas-sive erosion in the uplands and accelerated reservoir sedimentation in the valleys (as is reported for the Ambuklao reservoir in the Philippines [Chanco 1981]).

The mistake in pointing the finger of blame at shifting agricultures (e.g., swidden, kaingin, milpa, conuco, jhum, bush fallow, slash-and-burn) is a semantic one. In its traditional meaning, the label applied to a system of forest cutting, cropping, and fallowing that was sustainable because the cultivator was a long-term resident in one place and the cropping area was rotated (shifted) in the surrounding area. The fallow period was long enough in secondary forest to permit rebuilding of the nutrient budget on one site prior to its again being cut (and usually burned) for the next cropping period. With relatively low population density, low technology, and a subsistence economy, these were stable systems, ecologically well adapted to the tropical environment. Even on fairly steep slopes, the small area of soil disturbed in order to plant and cultivate annual crops accelerated erosion only slightly. The small area cultivated at any one time (typically less than 3 percent of the total area) in relation to the mosaic fallow area also meant that any soil moving from the cultivated area was usually trapped by the fallow, and sediment levels in streams did not necessarily increase in response to shifting agriculture (see Chapter 2). Many tribal peoples in the tropics are still practicing this *stable* system, though they represent a decreasing minority when compared to a more recently developed *unstable* system, which is also referred to as "shifting agriculture." The distinction between these systems has been clearly identified by Watters (1971) and by Kundstadter and Chapman (1978).

The newer system is an outgrowth of increased population pressure, landlessness, increased technology, and a shift to cash cropping rather than subsistence. These new shifting agriculturists are indeed often true shifters or migrants in that they move into a new area, clear it by slash-and-burn methods in substantially larger blocks, cultivate it until it is worn out, and then they move on to a new area. They are, in essence, perennial "new colonists" attacking the edge of the pristine forest and leaving behind degraded land that has suffered serious erosion because soil conservation methods are not part of the strategy of the landless and poor. Moreover, since there seldom is a mosaic of uncut forest and fallow patches of scrub, much of the eroded soil does move into stream channels as sediment and causes a host of adverse consequences.

It is inappropriate to group these two different systems under one blanket term and to attribute the well-documented environmental ills of one system to both. This has had disastrous consequences for tribal peoples in many parts of the tropical world. They have sometimes been evicted from their lands in the public domain in the name of preventing forest, soil, and water degradation. A more humane, thoughtful, and ecologically sound strategy might be to assist them gradually to improve their practices, perhaps in an agroforestry context, with the introduction of new food tree crops. A recent program of forest occupancy management begun in the Philippines is indeed an important step in this direction (Duldulao 1981). Let us be more precise in our language when discussing erosion and sedimentation from shifting agriculture. Even with the unstable form of shifting agriculture, the erosion consequences may be somewhat overrated, or it may be at least dwarfed by the erosion resulting from road construction, urban development, drainage outlets, and other civil engineering, rather than agronomic, activities (Sanchez 1979).

GRASSLAND IS BETTER COVER FOR WATERSHEDS THAN FOREST?

In forest watershed research, it has been shown in several experiments that conversion of forest to grass as the dominant cover has usually resulted in greater water yield (e.g., Hibbert 1969, Queensland Department of Forestry 1977), higher groundwater levels in deep soils (Boughton 1970, Melzer 1962) with only small increases or no increases in stormflow volume, peakflows, or storm duration flow, depending on grass density and productivity (Hibbert 1969, Helvey and Douglass 1971, Queensland Department of Forestry 1977). The grasslands in these instances were not grazed, for the experiments were designed to compare the hydrologic effects of the different vegetative covers. Once the grass was established, there was no difference in erosion rates or sediment production from the area (Coster 1938, Helvey and Douglass 1971).

Some politicians, water development engineers, and planners have read or heard about these results and suggested that grass would be a better cover than trees on watersheds because increased water yields in streams and rivers are important in water projects for water supply, hydro power, and irrigation. They have been told that deep-rooted forests are heavy users of water, and now they suggest replacing them with grasslands that use less water but still give hydrologic safety. Such a policy, if widely adopted, would be inappropriate for at least two important reasons.

First, these experiments were conducted on moderate slopes not prone to mass wasting. The importance of tree root shear strength in maintaining slope stability on steepland areas prone to landslip and slumping has now been well documented (for example, O'Loughlin 1974). On such areas, forest cover gives the greatest protection against this most damaging form of erosion and its corresponding increase in sedimentation.

In addition, these aforementioned experimental results were obtained from grasslands that were not grazed and not burned. In actual practice in the tropics, any area of grassland is likely to be grazed, and usually overgrazed, and is also likely to be burned to maintain it in grass. While controlled grazing and prescribed burning at appropriate intervals need not have serious adverse impacts on the hydrology and soils of a watershed, such control is practically impossible to achieve in most tropical countries where populations are increasing rapidly and food production needs are high. Overgrazing and indiscriminate burning, especially over long periods, result in a well-known series of adverse hydrologic and soil movement effects (Cochrane 1969, Raeder-Roitzsch and Masur 1968). The extensive degraded grasslands of the tropics are unravelling testimony to this situation.

Forests are hydrologically and erosionally safer because they are less susceptible to intensive use — as long as they are maintained as forestlands. Harvesting minor forest products from them has an insignificant effect on watershed values (see Chapter 1). Commercial wood harvesting, even when clearcutting is involved, is carried out at relatively infrequent intervals compared with continuous grazing, and any hydrologic or soil impacts are rather quickly restored to preharvest levels (at least in the more humid tropics) through vegetation regrowth. Of some concern, however, to watershed relationships will be the increasing emphasis on plantations of rapidly growing trees that are harvested totally, with large equipment, on very short rotations, as either chips for pulp or for bioenergy.

REFORESTATION OR AFFORESTATION WILL STOP FLOODS, AMELIORATE DROUGHTS, CAUSE STREAMS TO FLOW AGAIN AND RAISE WATER LEVELS IN WELLS?

Large-scale programs of reforestation or afforestation are being called for and to some extent carried out in tropical watersheds of most countries. As a strategy to establish "wood factories" to meet needs for fuel, timber, and other wood products, this makes good sense. Hopefully it will relieve some of the pressure on remaining bits of natural forest. Moreover, as a rehabilitation device to make unproductive lands more productive, to minimize erosion, and to rebuild nutrient budgets, such efforts are indeed well conceived. The fuzziness appears when the clarion call goes out that through planting trees, rainfall will increase (droughts cease), springs, wells, and streams will flow once more, and floods will be prevented.

In most respects, putting trees back on open land (reforestation) or planting them on areas long without or never with forest (afforestation) produces the opposite effects to taking trees off. The effects of forest cutting have been discussed previously but will be summarized here in terms of reverse effects. There is no evidence that planting forests will increase rainfall except in those special cases of physiography where fog or cloud capture of moisture may result. In those special circumstances, establishment of forest may result in additional *effective* precipitation, which under many geologic and soil situations will appear as increased groundwater and baseflow. While this does not influence local or regional rainfall, it may therefore improve well levels and springs and increase stream yields, including low-season flows. In most experiments, however, reforestation of open land has resulted in lower water tables, less reliable springs, and reduced streamflow, especially in the dry season (Banks and Kromhout 1963, and others cited in Chapter 12). An example of the policy dilemma has occurred recently in Fiji, where contrary to conventional wisdom and expectations of a decade ago, the large reforestation program of the Fiji Pine Commission is resulting in decreased streamflows (Drysdale 1981, Pers. Comm.). And finally, while stormflows may be somewhat reduced, most experiments have shown rather small effects (Hewlett 1982). Certainly for major floods on the lower reaches of rivers, it is doubtful if there is much impact of even rather large-scale forest planting programs, *unless* a major portion of the catchment was in a degraded, severely gullied, soil compacted state, where almost all precipitation was quickly channeled to the streams and rivers, out where sediment derived from upland erosion was a major contributor to flooding. In such cases (and there are many landscapes in the hilly tropics that have been so abused they would seem to qualify), the establishment of forests might indeed slow and reduce surface runoff to the point where there would be some flood *reduction* effect, though not elimination of floods. It would certainly reduce erosion rates and resulting contribution to river sediments.

CONCLUSION

Problems in achieving sustainable development and conservation of soil and water resources in the tropics are legion enough, without being plagued by myth, misunderstanding, misinformation, and misinterpretation. Semantic fuzziness adds to the scene. Words such as deforestation, shifting agriculture, marginal lands, and desertification usually need to be defined or avoided in favor of more precise words or phrases. The consequences may be seen in fruitless disagreement between interest groups, propaganda instead of education, bad policymaking because of shaky scientific bases, or even good policymaking for the wrong reasons—an action that may backfire. Perhaps foresters have been guilty of aquiescing by silence to the use of some misinterpretations and misunderstandings, because the arguments or rhetoric being used were aimed at protecting forest resources or at establishing new forests—surely actions worthy of nations and statesmen. But, if we close the watershed forests to human use and reservoirs still silt up, and when we have totally reclothed the basin in planted forest and we still have floods, and if on top of that the streams still dry up or dry up even more . . . then there may be a well-deserved backlash and the credibility of foresters and other watershed professionals may be called into serious question. There are many eminently sound reasons for forest conservation and reforestation in the tropical developing countries. Let us not condone the use of unsupportable or questionable hydrologic and erosional relationships in this important policy scenario.

Appendix A
Workshop Participants

Johari Baharudin
Assistant Director (Natural Forests)
　Forest Research Institute
　Kepong, MALAYSIA

Michael Bonell
Lecturer, Physical Geography
　Department of Geography
　James Cook University of North Queensland
　Qld 48811, AUSTRALIA

Herbert Bormann
Professor
　School of Forestry and Environmental Studies
　Yale University
　New Haven, CT 06511 U.S.A.

Walter C. Boughton
Senior Lecturer
　School of Australian Environmental Studies
　Griffith University
　Nathan, Brisbane Qld 4111, AUSTRALIA

David Cassells
Forest Hydrologist
　Queensland Department of Forestry
　Research Center
　Gympie, Qld 4570, AUSTRALIA

Kasem Chunkao
Associate Professor
　Department of Conservation
　Faculty of Forestry
　Kasetsart University
　Bangkok, THAILAND

134

James Douglass
Project Leader
  Coweeta Hydrologic Lab
  U.S. Forest Service
  Box 216
  Otto, NC 28763 U.S.A.

Peter Drysdale
Manager, Forestry Division
  Fiji Pine Commission
  Box 521
  Lautoka, FIJI

Samir El-Swaify
Professor
  Dept. of Agronomy and Soils
  University of Hawaii
  Honolulu, HI 96822 U.S.A.

Lawrence Hamilton
Research Associate
  East-West Environment and Policy Institute
  1777 East-West Road
  Honolulu, HI 96848 U.S.A.

Yuan-lin Lin
Consultant, Watershed
  Taiwan Forestry Research Institute
  53 Nan-Hai Road
  Taipei, Taiwan, CHINA

Low Kwai Sim
Associate Professor
  Department of Geography
  University of Malaysia
  Kuala Lumpur 22-11
  MALAYSIA

Syafii Manan
Senior Lecturer
  Department of Forest Management
  Faculty of Forestry
  Bogor Agricultural University, IPB
  P.O. Box 69
  Bogor, Java
  INDONESIA

Harley Manner
Lecturer in Geography
  School of Social and Economic Development
  University of the South Pacific
  P.O. Box 1168
  Suva, FIJI

Walter F. Megahan
Principal Research Hydrologist
  U.S. Forest Service
  Intermountain Forest and Range Experiment Station
  Forestry Sciences Laboratory
  316 East Myrtle Street
  Boise, ID 83702 U.S.A.

Colin L. O'Loughlin
Head, Geohydrology Section
  Forest Research Institute
  P.O. Box 31-011
  Christchurch, NEW ZEALAND

Jemuel Perino
Division Chief
  Watershed and Range Research Division
  Forest Research Institute
  College, Laguna, PHILIPPINES 3720

Samarn Rouysungnern
Chief of Research Section
  Watershed Management Division
  Royal Forest Department
  Bangkhen, Bangkok 9, THAILAND

Severo Saplaco
Professor
  Department of Forest Management
  University of the Philippines at Los Banos
  College, Laguna, PHILIPPINES

Yoshinori Tsukamoto
Professor
  Department of Forestry
  Tokyo University of Agriculture and Technology
  Saiwaicho 3-5-8, Fuchu, Tokyo 183
  JAPAN

Napoleon Vergara
Research Associate
  East-West Environment and Policy Institute
  1777 East-West Road
  Honolulu, HI 96848 U.S.A.

Les Whitmore
Forester
  U.S.D.A. Forest Service (IF)
  P.O. Box 2417
  Washington, DC 20013 U.S.A.

Hulton Wood
Institute of Pacific Island Forestry
  U.S.D.A. Forest Service
  Honolulu, HI 96813 U.S.A.

Frank Zadroga
Regional Specialist
  Oficina Regional para Programas de Centro America
  ROCAP
  8A Calle 7-86, zona 9
  Guatemala City, GUATEMALA

Appendix B
A Summary of Some Results from the Coweeta Hydrologic Laboratory*

The Effects of Tree Cutting and Timber Harvesting on Timing and Distribution of Water Yield

The Coweeta Basin is located in western North Carolina in the Blue Ridge Province of the Appalachian Highlands Physiographic Division; the basin is 1,625 ha in size, slopes at 18 percent to the east and varies from 685 to 1,592 m in elevation. Ridges are sharp-crested, valleys vary from V-shaped for subdrainages to broad U-shaped for the major valleys, and the drainage pattern is dendritic. Stream density is high, around 6 km/km².

The climate is classified as humid mesothermal with temperatures averaging 3.6°C in January and 21.6°C in July. Rainfall in the Coweeta vicinity is the highest in the eastern United States. It varies with elevation (slight orographic effect) from 1,768 mm at low elevations to 2,300 mm at high elevations and averages 2,058 mm annually.

Rainfall is distributed fairly evenly throughout the year, with March the highest rainfall month (210 mm) and October the lowest (160 mm). Storms average 133 events per year.

Under the warm, humid climate, rocks have weathered into a deep, permeable regolith. The deepest layers are generally found on ridges and in valleys; soil on side slopes is variable in depth ranging from rock outcrops to deep, porous material over 25 m deep.

Because of the mild, humid climate, vegetation at Coweeta is diverse. The forest is multistoried and composed of four forest types—northern hardwoods, cove hardwoods, oak-hickory, and pine-hardwoods. The dense understory is composed of tree saplings and usually an abundance of shrub species. Ground cover is also diverse.

At Coweeta, water yield is distributed seasonally with the monthly high normally in March. It declines progressively until October, when recharge begins. Cutting vegetation changes this distribution by increasing flow levels throughout the summer, fall, and winter. This was best demonstrated by Watershed 17, which was clearcut annually for seven years. The

* Contribution to Watershed Forest Influence Workshop, 1981, by Dr. James E. Douglass, Project Leader, Coweeta Hydrologic Laboratory, U.S. Forest Service, Otto, North Carolina, U.S.A.

monthly increase in streamflow was near zero in May, increased to a maximum of 39 mm in December and declined thereafter to near zero in March (Douglass and Swank 1975). Because of reduced evapotranspiration and higher soil moisture levels on the cut watershed, a difference in soil water storage exists. The potential increase in streamflow during any month is proportional to the storage difference. Rainfall converts the potential into a real difference in streamflow. The size of the increase during any month is thus dependent on both the accumulated soil moisture storage difference and current rainfall. At least 100 mm/month is required to produce an increase. Conversely, 300 mm or more of rain during one month after a dry summer can increase flow from a clearcut watershed by 50 to 70 mm.

Because of the deep soils at Coweeta, increases in streamflow from harvest of timber come during the season when flow is least and demand for water is greatest. The increases are delayed into the later winter, in sharp contrast to areas where soils are shallower. Elsewhere in the Appalachians, all evapotranspiration savings are usually recouped much earlier, normally by November, because shallow soils are recharged sooner. After maximum recharge, no difference in yield will occur.

A thorough examination of the effect of timber harvest on timing of yield has not been made for all experiments at Coweeta. Two conditions have been studied: the cutting of forest vegetation without road construction or logging, and harvesting of timber with the usual logging and road activities. In the former case, the physical properties of the hydrologic system are not changed; the rate of water movement through the system is simply accelerated.

Consider first the hydrograph of the undisturbed watershed that serves as a basis for measuring the response or change produced by management. Hibbert and Cunningham (1966) used computers to separate streamflow into stormflow and baseflow components, either of which might be changed by treatment. The advantages of using this method are consistency of separation and freedom from human bias. Hewlett and Hibbert (1967) used this technique to study stormflow factors affecting the response of small watersheds to rainfall. Stormflow response (mean percent of precipitation appearing as stormflow) was highly variable for forested watersheds in the eastern U.S., ranging from 2 to 34 percent. At Coweeta, the watershed response was 4 to 15 percent depending on soil depth, slope, and number and size of storms. Hewlett's (1967) detailed mapping of stormflow indicates an even larger response from shallow soils at higher elevations at Coweeta—up to 20 percent. Eighty-six percent of the variation in stormflow volume from one 7.7 km² Coweeta watershed was accounted for by precipitation (P), antecedent flow (I), season (S), and duration of the storm runoff (D) (Hewlett et al. 1977b). Surprisingly, adding rainfall intensity to the equation did not increase the percent variation in stormflow accounted for. Precipitation intensity was slightly more important when accounting for variations in peakflow; P, I, S, and D accounted for 72 percent and intensity variables accounted for another 4.7 percent of the variation in peak discharge.

Hewlett et al. (1977a) developed a model for predicting stormflow volumes and peaks from 11 forested watersheds from New Hampshire to South Carolina. Only the response factor (stormflow volume/precipitation volume) for the watershed, precipitation (P), flow rate at the beginning of the storm (I), and season (S) were significant factors determining stormflow. The addition of a precipitation intensity variable or precipitation-area interaction did not improve prediction. In these analyses, flow was expressed in $ft^3/sec/mi^2$; consequently, drainage area was not significant in determining runoff peaks or volumes.

Flood recurrence data on forested watersheds in the mountainous region of North Carolina is often needed for planning purposes (Douglass 1974). Peak discharge was estimated for 2-, 5-, 10-, 20-, 30-, 40-, and 50-year recurrence intervals from watershed area and maximum elevation ($r^2 > 0.98$). The elevation variable is highly significant and is thought to integrate the tendency for precipitation and land slope to increase and soil depth to decrease with elevation. For each 150 m increase in elevation, peak discharge for a given recurrence interval increases by 1.3 to 1.6. These equations are area specific and cannot be extrapolated to other areas. Helvey (1981), for example, observed significantly higher peak flows at a given elevation from forested watersheds in West Virginia, as might be expected for those shallower soils.

Thus, storm hydrographs of undisturbed watersheds have provided clues to the sources of runoff from forested land and a benchmark for measuring hydrograph changes caused by management. As will be shown, although the control watershed approach has been used in most analyses, the response factor of the watershed (percent of rainfall which appears as stormflow) is important in determining the size of the changes in storm hydrograph parameters; rainfall intensity appears less important.

Clearcutting a high-elevation, mature hardwood forest at Coweeta (Watershed 37) without removing forest products increased stormflow volume an average of 11 percent (0.58 cm at a mean flow of 5.33 cm). The increase varied from 0 for small storms to 22 percent for a regional record flood (Hewlett and Helvey 1970). These increases were produced without overland flow being a factor. The increase in stormflow for winter-spring storms was about half that produced by summer-fall storms (Helvey and Douglass 1971). Watersheds 13 and 17 were also clearcut without removal of forest products. Summer-fall storms also produced the greatest increase in stormflow on Watershed 13, almost 50 percent of stormflow of the control watershed. On Watershed 17, the stormflow increase averaged about 20 percent of the flow from its control. The tendency was for the stormflow increases to be greatest on lower-elevation, least-responsive watersheds both in absolute amounts and as a percentage. Increases of up to 40 mm of stormflow from low-elevation, low-response watersheds were produced by clearcutting compared to increases up to 25 mm from high-elevation, high-response watersheds. Thus, the increase in stormflow appears to be negatively correlated with the stormflow response of the watershed before cutting; that is, the greater the average stormflow before cutting, the smaller will be the increase in stormflow after cutting. The reasons are unclear, but when data from five cutting experiments at Coweeta were adjusted for differences in response of control watersheds to storm size and antecedent storage conditions, the response to cutting the forest was similar for all watersheds. There was, however, a seasonal effect with the maximum stormflow increases of 4 mm from summer-fall storms compared to about 20 mm for winter-spring storms. The difference appears to be due to rainfall intensity differences between seasons. When storm size, antecedent storage conditions, and the product of the 60-minute precipitation intensity times watershed area were considered, the increase in stormflow volume could be estimated accurately (multiple r of 0.84, standard error of estimaté 3.8 mm of stormflow) (Helvey and Douglass 1971).

When products are harvested over a road or skid trail network, the timing of flow will change even more. When 66 percent of the basal area of timber was carefully harvested by bulldozers over a properly designed and constructed road system on Watershed 28 (Hewlett and Douglass 1968), stormflow during the first four years of harvest and regrowth increased 17 percent (Douglass and Swank 1976) compared to an 11 percent increase for clearcutting without harvest on a nearby watershed (Hewlett and Helvey 1970). During the next five years, the increase in stormflow averaged 10 percent, and no increase was obvious nine years after harvest. The inference is that harvesting timber over very carefully constructed roads will increase stormflow more than simply felling trees and leaving them in place. Extrapolating this inference, we can conclude that poorly constructed roads and sloppy harvesting techniques would further aggravate the situation; the effect would be larger, but its magnitude is uncertain.

Cutting timber without removing forest products increases peak discharge 22 to 38 percent on low-response watersheds over the peakflow of the control watersheds (Helvey and Douglass 1971) compared to only 7 percent for high-response watersheds (Hewlett and Helvey 1970). At higher elevations, the increase in peak was better correlated with maximum 60-minutes intensity than with peak flow on the control watershed. In the experiment in which 66 percent of the basal area was cut and carefully harvested over a good road system (Watershed 28), peak discharge increased 33

141

percent during harvest (fourfold to fivefold greater than on a nearby clearcut watershed without harvest). This increase in peaks declined logarithmically with regrowth of vegetation, becoming nonsignificant or nearly so when the streamflow increase declined to zero. As in the case of stormflow volume, we can infer that the effect would have been even larger for lower quality logging and roads. How much larger is uncertain.

Storm duration in hours increased after clearcutting timber without harvest. The increase in storm duration tended to be inversely related to stormflow response factors; the largest increase in storm duration occurred on the low-response watersheds and the smallest increase on the high-response watersheds (Helvey and Douglass 1971). Hewlett and Helvey (1970) failed to detect a change in time to peak, recession time, or storm duration after clearcutting the highest stormflow response watershed at Coweeta (Watershed 37).

Changes in the flow rate at the beginning of the storm (initial flow rate) are indicative of changes in baseflow. In every experiment where annual flow increased, there was a tendency for the initial flow rate to increase. Conversely, treatments that reduced total flow, as in the conversion to pine, also reduced the initial flow rate. The effect is always greatest for summer-fall storms.

To summarize, the effects of cutting and harvesting timber on the storm hydrograph are cumulative. Stormflow volume, peak flow, and storm duration are all generally increased by cutting timber, and the size of the increase is negatively correlated with the response factor for the watershed. Carefully constructed roads and good harvest techniques produce larger increases in these hydrograph parameters than cutting vegetation alone. The effect is greatest during the harvest and declines logarithmically with time as vegetation regrows. Theoretically, all parameters except peak discharge will return to preharvest levels as water use by regrowing vegetation reaches a maximum. Peaks may be an exception if the road system produces a permanent increase in the rate of surface runoff delivered to the streams.

(See Over)

Appendix C
Guidelines for Reducing Negative
Impacts of Logging*

A variety of environmental impacts can occur from timber harvest (logging), such as changes in the total volume or peak rate of streamflow, changes in nutrient outflows from the site, impacts to wildlife, and changes in scenic values. However, the primary concern with timber harvest operations is often directed at the on-site damages caused by accelerated erosion and the possibility of associated downstream damages caused by sedimentation. The emphasis in this Appendix is on minimizing the erosion and sedimentation consequences of timber harvest and on protecting the streams through the use of buffer zones. Much of the material presented here is abstracted from articles by Gilmour (1977), Rice (1977), and Megahan (1977) in the FAO publication, "Guidelines for Watershed Management" (FAO 1977). Guides for spacing erosion control structures are based on the work of Kidd (1963). Other material exists as well and should be used as applicable, especially when it has been derived from local experience.

BASIC SOIL PROBLEMS

A list of dos and don'ts for timber harvest is based on experience in limited areas and may or may not be applicable at a specific site. However, some basic statements can be presented that have general application.

Surface erosion—is the most common (but not necessarily the most damaging) form of accelerated erosion and is manifested by sheet wash, rilling, and gullying. Three factors govern the amount of surface erosion: erosion forces, soil protection, and inherent erosion hazards. By increasing the potential for overland flow, reducing the total amount and continuity of protective cover on the soil, and disturbing soil organic layers thus exposing more erodible mineral soils, logging can accelerate surface erosion. Surface erosion rates tend to be highest immediately after disturbance and decrease over time in response to increased soil revegetation and season-

---

*Material prepared by Dr. Walter F. Megahan (Fellow, East-West Environment and Policy Institute and Principal Research Hydrologist, U.S. Forest Service) and James Schweithelm, Research Intern, East-West Environment and Policy Institute.

ing of the soil surface. Thus, it is critical that measures designed to control surface erosion be applied as soon as possible after disturbance.

Mass erosion — The concern with mass erosion here will be limited to the shallow, relatively rapid-moving group of landslides known as debris avalanches and torrents. This type of slide occurs on steep slopes usually greater than 30 degrees and involves the upper soil mantle above a water-impeding zone in the soil or the underlying bedrock. Much of slope stability in forested areas is imparted by tree roots. After logging, the dead roots gradually decay and lose their strength. Vegetation regrowth is relatively slow so that root strength reaches a minimum usually within the four to eight years after cutting. The area is most vulnerable to failure at this time, usually long after surface erosion problems have healed.

Sediment delivery and stream protection — Erosion can cause damages either on-site primarily because of losses in forest productivity, or off-site because of sedimentation impacts. Normally, off-site damages can be minimized by establishing buffer strips to catch sediment below the zone of disturbance or initiating special practices to hold eroded material on site such as slash windrows within the zone of disturbance. Buffer strips adjacent to stream channels provide benefits in addition to filtering sediments and nutrients. These include minimizing temperature changes, maintaining food supplies for the aquatic ecosystem, and maintaining a long-time source of forest debris for stabilizing channels.

COMMERCIAL LOGGING OPERATIONS

A commercial logging operation is usually designed by a forester who must consider what type of *silvicultural system* to use; the need for, and methods of, *slash disposal* and *site preparation;* and the type of *logging method* to use — all within the framework of minimizing costs and environmental impacts. Since slash disposal and site preparation are not used commonly in the tropics, they will not be treated in this Appendix. In those cases where these practices will be used, such as in converting native forest to forest plantation or in harvesting plantations with a view to replanting, Gilmour (1977) has presented useful guidelines.

The silvicultural system refers to the selection of trees to cut and includes removal of all trees (clearcutting) or only some of the trees (partial cutting systems such as seed tree, shelterwood, or selection cutting). Usually, stand regeneration is the primary reason for selecting a silvicultural system. However, economic considerations and environmental impacts also may be a concern.

The logging method is the timber harvest operation that includes felling the trees and cutting them into logs and transporting the logs from the stump to a temporary storage area (log landings) located at a nearby road, railroad, or water body for transportation to the mill. This latter operation, called yarding, is done in a variety of ways, including carrying or dragging by animals such as elephants, or with different types of machinery such as wheeled or crawler tractors. Many times, long cables powered by winches located at the log landing are used to remove the logs. Logs may be simply dragged across the ground (ground cable systems) or the cables may be suspended in the air so that logs are carried partially or totally above the ground for part or all of the distance (skyline systems). Airships, including large balloons or, more commonly, helicopters (aerial systems) are also used for log yarding in some locations.

SELECTION OF A SILVICULTURAL SYSTEM

For a given watershed, the two factors differentiating silvicultural practices are the relative volume of timber removed and the size of openings created in the timber stand. Ranging from large to small, opening sizes tend to array as follows: clearcutting, seed tree, shelterwood cutting, group selection, and individual tree selection. The total volume of timber removed depends on the amount of watershed area affected. For example, a greater volume of timber might be removed by an individual selection cut over an entire watershed compared with a clearcut on only 20 percent of the area. However, the impact of the clearcut on surface erosion might be greater because of more complete and severe soil disturbance on the area affected. Other things being equal, the hydrologic impacts of partial cutting are less than for clearcutting for a given volume of timber removal. However, other things may not be equal. For example, more roads may be needing for the partial cutting systems.

Some guides for selection of silvicultural systems for minimizing erosion include:

1. Use partial cutting systems, preferably with as small an opening size as possible, in areas of high landslide hazard. Do not cut in known water accumulation areas, especially topographic depressions.
2. If clearcutting in high landslide hazard areas is required for regeneration purposes, leave undisturbed areas in known water accumulation areas, especially in topographic depressions. Middle and lower slope locations also should be avoided if possible.
3. Avoid clearcutting above roads in areas of high landslide hazard.
4. Leave buffer strips below clearcuts.
5. Avoid clearcutting a large proportion of individual watersheds whenever possible.
6. Maintain the size of clearcut units as small as possible.

SELECTION OF A HARVEST SYSTEM

Roads are required for almost all logging operations and are an important factor influencing the overall erosion impact. Erosion rates per unit area of disturbance have repeatedly been shown to be much greater on roads than on adjacent logged areas, often differing by one or two orders of magnitude (Megahan 1981). However, the total amount of erosion from roads compared with that caused by logging depends on the relative erosion rates for the two types of disturbances and the amount of area involved in each. For example, McCashion and Rice (1983) reported on a study comparing total erosion from a 12,271 ha area in California. Even though road erosion rates averaged 17 times greater than erosion rates on logged areas, the area affected by roads was much less, so only about 40 percent of the total erosion for the area was attributed to roads; the rest was caused by logging. Road erosion control practices are specific and detailed and will be found in Megahan (1977).

Total road construction varies with the type of harvest system. Megahan (1981) summarized the results of 16 studies in the United States and Canada, reporting on the amount of soil disturbance caused by alternative logging systems as an index of erosion potential (Appendix Figure C-1). The total disturbance averages greatest for tractor logging followed by ground cable. The amount of roads required for the tractor and cable systems is about 13 and 11 percent, respectively; the amount of disturbance caused by the logging equipment is the primary cause for the differences in total disturbance from the two logging systems. Many times, tractors cause severe soil mixing and soil compaction that may aggravate surface erosion in excess of cable logging systems. Rice and Datzman (1980) found that erosion per unit area of disturbance for tractor logging was 3.7 times greater than erosion per unit area of cable logging in northern California. Considering the difference in area disturbed by yarding for the two logging systems, the average tractor logging operation causes about 6 times more erosion than the average cable logging operation, assuming that the 3.7 factor is applicable to average conditions. Actually, the difference is even greater because of the larger average percentage of roads required for tractor logging (13 percent) compared to cable logging (11 percent).

No data were presented to evaluate animal yarding systems. However, road requirements are probably similar to that required for tractor logging. In contrast, the amount and severity of logging disturbance is undoubtedly less than that for tractor logging because of reduced skid trail width, depth of disturbance, and compaction.

Total soil disturbance from skyline logging is less than half that for ground cable logging. The largest part of the reduction is due to the more limited road system required for skyline logging—only 2 percent of the

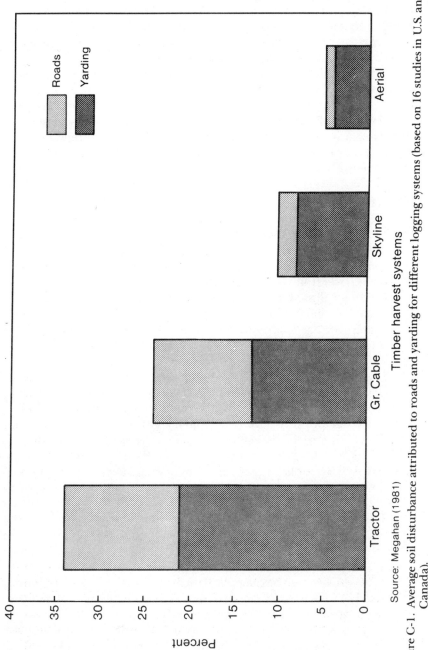

Source: Megahan (1981)

Timber harvest systems

Figure C-1. Average soil disturbance attributed to roads and yarding for different logging systems (based on 16 studies in U.S. and Canada).

area as compared with 10 percent for ground cable systems. Considering the higher unit area erosion rates on roads, the erosional advantage of selecting skyline over ground cable systems is apparent. Aerial logging operations are even more advantageous because the amount of disturbance by both logging and roads is about half that for skyline systems.

METHODS OF YARDING LOGS

Plan thoroughly and then yard the logs carefully in order to prevent soil disturbances and other water pollution hazards along skid trails, on landings, and over the watershed in general. Guidelines for yarding logs for minimal impact include:

1. Whenever possible, yard logs uphill rather than down (Appendix Figure C-2). Uphill yarding has been found to reduce erosion both in tractor harvesting and ground cable harvesting operations. In uphill yarding, log decks are placed on ridge or hill tops rather than in low-lying areas. This produces a skid trail pattern that disperses rather than concentrates surface runoff.
2. Correlate all skid trail locations with cutting areas, topography, soil types, and climatic factors. Locate trails carefully and drain them adequately so that muddy waters will be kept out of stream channels. Keep all skid trails out of stream channels and off stream banks. Use temporary log or metal culverts wherever such trails must cross stream channels, and keep the number of such crossings as few as possible. Use each skid trail only a small number of times in order to avoid soil gouging and compacting and the channelizing of runoff.
3. Avoid tractor yarding on all saturated areas and on all slopes steeper than 30 percent. On critical soils, limit crawler-tractor yarding to slopes of less than 25 percent.
4. Suspend tractor logging during rainy days and for a day or so thereafter. Store logs ahead of the loading operation to allow for yarding shutdowns on bad days.
5. Locate log landing areas on firm, dry ground away from live stream channels wherever possible. Design landings so they will drain into well-vegetated buffer areas.
6. Wherever possible, yard logs by lifting them free of the ground. Where this cannot be done, yard them uphill by high-lead cable or by fixed or swinging skyline. Protect all stream banks and channels by bridging or at least by lifting the logs over streams rather than dragging them through the streams. Avoid disturbing steep slopes and shallow soil areas immediately adjacent to stream channels. Avoid undue disturbances of accumulations of decaying vegetation that can wash into and befoul the streams during rainstorms.

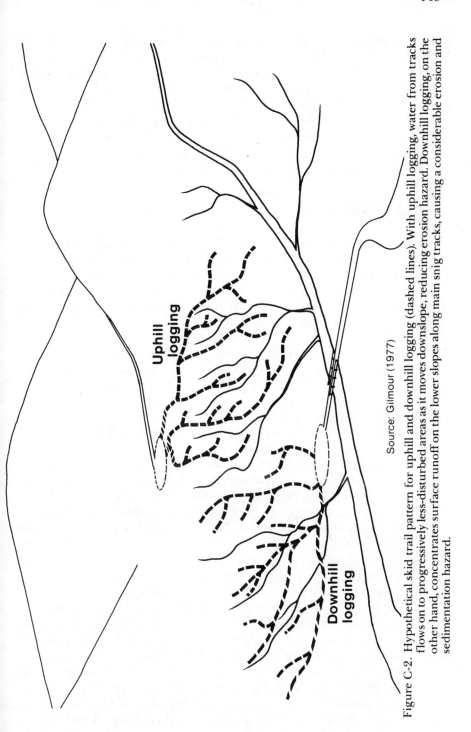

Figure C-2. Hypothetical skid trail pattern for uphill and downhill logging (dashed lines). With uphill logging, water from tracks flows on to progressively less-disturbed areas as it moves downslope, reducing erosion hazard. Downhill logging, on the other hand, concentrates surface runoff on the lower slopes along main snig tracks, causing a considerable erosion and sedimentation hazard.

7. Minimize logging road construction on very steep slopes or fragile areas by using skyline or balloon yarding systems.

8. Consider the use of helicopters, balloons, or modified cable systems for logging areas that would have high conventional yarding costs or for fragile, sensitive areas.

9. Take all possible care to avoid damage to the soils of forested slopes, and to the soil and water of natural meadows as well. Minimize this damage by operating the logging equipment only when soil moisture conditions are such that excessive damage will not result.

BUFFER STRIPS

Soil erosion on, and logging debris from, roads, landings, skidways, and slopes disturbed by yarding activities during a logging operation can seriously damage streams. Much of this damage can be prevented by keeping roads and logging activity as far from the stream courses as possible. Therefore, leave buffer strips of native vegetation, including an overhead canopy, between roads or logged areas, and any perennial streams they parallel. Buffer strips not only reduce the quantity of sediment and logging wastes that reach the streams, but also help maintain the integrity of the aquatic ecosystem as well. Guidelines for maintaining buffer strips include:

1. Leave all trees, shrubs, grasses, rocks, and natural "down" timber wherever they afford shade over a perennial stream or maintain the integrity of the soil near such a stream.

2. Leave the buffer strip undisturbed. If trees must be removed, carefully and selectively log the timber from the buffer strip in such a way that shading and filtering effects are not destroyed. Protect buffer strips by leaving stumps high enough to prevent any subsequently felled, up-slope trees from sliding or rolling through the strips and into the streams.

3. Although neither an optimum nor a minimum width can be set arbitrarily for buffer strips, it is recommended that a minimum width of 25 meters on each side of the stream be used as a guide for establishing buffer strips. At the same time it must be realized that the necessary width will vary with steepness of the terrain, the nature of the undercover, the kind of soil, and the amount of timber to be removed.

4. For effective filtering of sediment, establish buffer strips that are wide enough to entrap the material that will be eroded from the road or the logged area above. Under some conditions and with careful control in adjacent logging areas, a relatively narrow strip may suffice. On the other hand, where road building or logging allows land slips

to occur, the buffer strip may have to be much wider and other precautions may have to be taken to eliminate adverse effects on the stream water quality.

5. For a modified buffer strip plan, remove only dead, dying, mature, and high-risk trees from the area. Trees should be felled away from the stream whenever possible. Debris within the channel or probable flood zone should be removed carefully.

6. Where old growth timber must be removed because it is subject to windthrow and where it is difficult to leave full-width buffer strips of timber to shade the stream, plan to re-establish cover along the stream after cutting is completed. Fast-growing species will be required to restore shade as quickly as possible. In the meantime, leaving the understory vegetation as undisturbed as possible will filter the runoff and stabilize the soil.

7. Many relatively small tributary streams flow only during the wet season of the year; however, they often produce substantial flows which carry heavy sediment loads during intense or prolonged periods of rain. Along the channels of intermittent tributaries, preserve adequate widths of undergrowth vegetation as filter strips to prevent washing of sediment into a perennial stream below.

WATERSHED RESTORATION

Many times, site damages occur in spite of all good intentions to avoid them. Other times, damages are anticipated with the idea that restoration measures will be taken to mitigate them. Areas of concern include the general area logged, skid trails, landings, and fire lines.

LOGGED AREAS

Clearcut logging and yarding operations and the handling and disposal of logging slash disturb drastically the land surface of steep mountain slopes. Guidelines for mitigating this disturbance include:

1. Control the erosion at its source on such disturbed areas by hastening their reforestation.
2. Seed or plant adapted species and, where necessary, use terracing, composting, mulching, and fertilizing.

SKID TRAILS

Guidelines for mitigating skid trail impacts include:

1. Restore stream channels by removing temporary skid-trail crossings.

2. Obliterate and stabilize all skid trails after logging the watershed by mulching and reseeding.
3. If necessary, build cross drains on abandoned skid roads to protect stream channels or side slopes in addition to mulching and reseeding. Be sure spacing is close enough for the slope gradient and type of soil involved. Lacking local guidelines, a spacing based on the following relationship is recommended: Spacing $= 87 - 1.8S + 0.0105S^2$ where S is slope gradient in percent.

LANDINGS

For landings, guidelines include:

1. Locate log loading or log landing areas along ridge tops, on other areas having gentle slopes, or along widened road areas.
2. Place landings in the channels of intermittent streams only in those emergency situations where no safe alternative location can be found. Adequately drain any landing that must be placed in such channels. Immediately after completing all log loadings from these landings, clear the channel to its full capacity, spread the fill material in areas where it will remain stable, and reseed those areas to herbaceous vegetation.
3. Upon abandonment, "erosion-proof" all landings by adequately ditching or mulching them with forest litter, as needed. Establish a herbaceous cover on those areas that will be used again in repeated cutting cycles, and restock to coniferous species those landings, located in clear-cut areas, that will not be reused for a long time.

FIRELINES

Guidelines for firelines include:

1. Limit tractor-built firelines to areas where they will not involve problems of soil instability.
2. Adequately "cross-ditch" all firelines at time of construction and revegetate them with adapted grasses and legumes using the same spacing as on skid roads.

PUTTING THE GUIDELINES INTO PRACTICE

From a practical point of view, individual areas should be assessed when they are first considered for logging, so that conditions can be inserted into timber sale agreements aimed at keeping erosion and stream sedimentation to a minimum. The conditions will depend on local environmental factors such as vegetation, geology, soil, topography and rainfall regime. Water end use also needs to be considered. For example, more stringent conditions will need to be applied in domestic water supply catchments than in areas where the water has no significant downstream use.

This assessment of individual areas is essential because of the widely varying conditions even within relatively small areas. For example, a logging practice that is acceptable in one area may be quite unacceptable in another adjacent area because of a change in the soil parent material from a stable sediment to a highly dispersive granite.

The assessment of areas before logging and the determination of special conditions to be applied to those areas means a substantial element of pre-planning for the entire logging operation. The type of logging (uphill or downhill); the location of roads, skid trails, and log landings; the location and type of stream crossings; and the type of machinery to be used should all be decided before the operation begins. This involves a rather radical change from routine practice in many areas, where "logger's choice" is the rule rather than the exception. However, it is a necessary change to keep the environmental impacts of logging to a minimum. This can be accomplished by developing a logging plan. Timber sale contracts should stipulate that a logging plan be prepared before the harvesting operation begins. The plan may be prepared by the operator, by government foresters, or jointly. The plan should be analyzed carefully by someone competent to judge the technical aspects of the plan and its environmental impacts. The operator should not be permitted to enter the harvest area until the plan has been approved. The sale contract should make provision for frequent inspections of the logging operation and empower the watershed manager to halt logging for noncompliance with the plan or other contract stipulations.

An adequate tree-harvesting plan includes maps, sketches, or pictures of the area to be harvested. It gives specifications for the building, use, and maintenance of a well-designed transportation system. It specifies the manner in which the trees are to be cut and the way the logs will be delivered to the transportation system from the watershed point where they are felled. It identifies the areas along perennial and major intermittent streams that should be left as buffer or filter strips. It specifies the measures that should be taken to leave the logged area in a repaired condition to prevent undue erosion during the period of regrowth.

In spite of the need to lay down detailed conditions for each sale area, it is desirable to maintain a certain degree of flexibility so that on-the-spot decisions can be made to take account of particular circumstances; e.g., it may be decided that a tree just within a buffer strip can be cut without causing any damage to soil or water values while another tree some distance outside a buffer strip should be left uncut (possibly because it was leaning toward the stream on a steep slope). Such flexibility throws the onus on individuals who must take responsibility for their decisions; they can't hide behind the regulations. This means, of course, that field operators must be skilled and well trained. Persons responsible for administering the timber sale need to keep in mind that proper execution of the sale requires close coordination with the timber operator. In order to accomplish this, it is necessary to appreciate the capabilities of the logger and the equipment and the technical and economic constraints under which the logger must operate.

It is generally easier to include "conditions" ("conditions" referring to restrictions, guidelines, specifications, etc.) in timber sale agreements than to get them applied. Field operators (both public forestry and private) tend to be conservative and resist change. It is reasonably easy to convince both the forestry profession and timber industry leaders of the need for change. This awareness has then to be passed on to the people in the field who are actually doing the job—forest rangers and overseers, timber cutters, and haulers. This is probably the most difficult part and it requires great patience and perseverance by the supervisors. If the supervisors do their jobs well and convince the field operators of the benefits of the changed conditions, the time will come when field personnel will be conscious of water and soil values as well as timber values and will automatically "do the right thing."

155

References

Anonymous. 1980. Rules on harvesting, cutting of rattan out; rattan incentives out. *The Philippine Lumberman* 26(7):30.
Anonymous. 1981. How trees can combat droughts and floods. *World Water*, October, p. 18.
Apolo, W. 1979. The control of run-off and erosion by sylvo-pastoral systems. *Proc. Workshop Agro-Forestry Systems in Latin America*, CATIE, Turrialba, pp. 184–86.
Avery, D. 1978. Firewood in the less developed countries. Eighth World Forestry Congress. IUFRO. Voluntary Paper. Agenda Item 3. Jakarta.
Ball, J. B. 1981. An evaluation of land-clearing methods for forest plantations in Nigeria. In *Tropical Agricultural Hydrology*, ed. R. Lal and E. W. Russell, pp. 111–17. New York: John Wiley and Sons.
Banks, C. H., and C. Kromhout. 1963. The effect of afforestation with *Pinus radiata* on summer baseflow and total annual discharge from Jonkershoek catchments. *Forestry in South Africa* 3: 43–65.
Bell, F. C., and M. T. Gatenby. 1969. Effects of exotic softwood afforestation on water yield. Water Resources Foundation Australia, Bull. 15, Canberra.
Bell, T. I. W. 1973. Erosion in the Trinidad teak plantations. *Commonwealth Forestry Review* 52:223–33.
Bell, T. I. W. and T. Evo. 1982. Energy plantations in the Fiji dry zone. Fiji Pine Research Paper 10. Suva and Lautoka.
Bermudez, M. 1979. Hydrological erosion and the occurrence of weeds in agro-forestry systems: The case of a coffee plantation with *Cordia alliodora* in Florencia Sur, Costa Rica. *Proc. Workshop Agro-Forestry Systems in Latin America*, CATIE, Turrialba, p. 187.
Blackie, J. R. 1972. Hydrological effects of a change in land use from rain forest to tea plantation in Kenya. *Proc. Symp. Representative and Experimental Basins*, Publ. 92, vol. 2, pp. 312–29, Wellington: UNESCO/IASH
Bormann, F. H., and G. E. Likens. 1981. Pattern and process in a forested ecosystem. New York: Springer-Verlag.
Bosch, J. M., and J. D. Hewlett. 1980. Sediment control in South African forests and mountain catchments. *South African Forestry* 115:50–55.

156

Bosch, J. M., and J. D. Hewlett. 1982. A review of catchment experiments to determine the effect of vegetation changes on water yield and evapotranspiration. *Hydrology* 55:3–23.

Boughton, W. C. 1970. Effects of and management on quantity and quality of available water: A review. Australian Water Resources Council Research Project 68/2, Report 120. Manly Vale: University of New South Wales.

Brasell, H. M., G. L. Unwin, and G. C. Stocker. 1980. The quantity, temporal distribution and mineral-element content of litterfall in two forest types at two sites in tropical Australia. *Ecology* 68:123–139.

Brown, J. A. H. 1972. Hydrologic effects of bushfire in a catchment in Southeast New South Wales. *Hydrology* 15:77–96.

Bruijnzeel, L. A. 1982. Hydrological and biochemical aspects of man-made forests in South-Central Java, Indonesia. Amsterdam: Free University of Amsterdam.

Brunig, E. F., M. von Buch, J. Heuveldop, and K. F. Panzer. 1975. Stratification of the tropical moist forest for land use planning. *Plant Research and Development* 2:21–44.

Budowski, G. 1981. Applicability of agroforestry systems. *International Workshop on Agroforestry in the African Humid Tropics*, Ibadan. Reproduced CATIE, Turrialba.

Burbridge, P., J. A. Dixon, and B. Soewardi. 1981. Forestry and agriculture: Options for resource allocation in choosing lands for transmigration development. *Applied Geography* 1: 237–58.

Burgess, F. F. 1973. The impact of commercial forestry on the hill forests of the Malay Peninsula. *Proc. Symposium on Biological Resources and National Development*, Kuala Lumpur, pp. 131–36.

Cassells, D. S., D. A. Gilmour, and P. Gordon. 1982. The impact of plantation forestry on stream sedimentation in tropical and sub-tropical Queensland—An initial assessment. *Proc. Conference on Agricultural Engineering*, Inst. of Engineers, Australia. (In Press)

Cassells, D., L. S. Hamilton, and S. R. Saplaco. 1982. Understanding the role of forests in watershed protection. Honolulu: East-West Center Environment and Policy Institute Working Paper.

Castellanos, V., and J. L. Thames. 1980. Application of multiple-use research on watersheds in Honduras. Paper presented at IUFRO/MAB Conference: Research in Multiple Use of Forest Resources, Flagstaff. p. 93–96.

Chinnamani, S. 1975. Soil conservation under perennial vegetation on hills. *Planters' Chronicle* 70:128–29.

Chanko, M. 1981. Ambuklao reservoir is good for only 1½ years. *Evening Post* (Manila), Jan. 12.

Chorley, J. L., and S. W. Cowling. 1968. Changes in soil nutrient status resulting from overgrazing and their consequences in plant communities of semi-arid areas. *Proc. Ecological Soc. Australia* 3(?):28–38.

Clarke, W. C. 1966. From extensive to intensive shifting cultivation: A succession from New Guinea. *Ethnology* 5:347–59.

Cochrane, G. R. 1969. Problems of vegetation change in Western Viti Levu, Fiji. In *Settlement and Encounter: Geographical Studies Presented to Sir Grenfell Price*, ed. F. Gale and G. H. Lawton, pp. 115–47. Melbourne: Oxford University Press.

Combe, J., and G. Budowski. 1979. Classification of agro-forestry techniques. *Proc. Workshop Agro-Forestry Systems in Latin America*, CATIE, Turrialba, pp. 17–47.

Cooke, J. G. 1980. Land use in relation to water quantity and quality. In *Proc. Seminar on Land Use in Relation to Water Quantity and Quality*. Nelson Catchment Board Publication, Nelson, N.Z.

Corvera, A. K. 1981. What caused the great Agusan Flood? *Weekend*, March 1, 1981. pp. 12-13.

Coster, C. 1938. Surficial runoff and erosion in Java. *Tectona* 31:613–728.

Couper, D. C., R. Lal, and S. L. Classen. 1981. Land clearing and development for agricultural purposes in Western Nigeria. In *Tropical Agricultural Hydrology*, ed. R. Lal and E. W. Russell, pp. 119–30. New York: John Wiley and Sons.

di Castri, F., and M. Hadley. 1979. A typology of scientific bottlenecks to natural resources development. *Geo.*, 3.6:513–22.

Dils, R. E. 1953. Influence of forest cutting and mountain farming on some vegetation, surface soil and surface runoff characteristics. U.S.D.A. Forest Service Paper 24, Southeastern Forest Expt. Sta., Asheville, N.C.

Douglas, I. 1967. Natural and man-made erosion in the humid tropics of Australia, Malaysia, and Singapore. International Assoc. Hydrological Sciences Publ. 75, Washington, pp. 17–30.

Douglass, J. E. 1974. Flood frequencies and bridge and culvert sizes for forested mountains of North Carolina. U.S.D.A. Forest Service Gen. Tech. Rept. SE-4, Asheville, N.C.

Douglass, J. E. 1981. Watershed experiments by the Coweeta Hydrologic Laboratory. Unpublished paper given to Watershed Forest Influence Workshop, East-West Center, Honolulu.

Douglass, J. E., and W. T. Swank. 1972. Streamflow modification through management of eastern forests. U.S.D.A. Forest Service Southeastern Forest Expt. Sta. Research Paper SE-94, Asheville, N.C.

Douglass, J. E., and W. T. Swank. 1975. Effects of management practices on water quality and quantity: Coweeta Hydrologic Laboratory, North Carolina. In *Municipal Watershed Management Symposium Proc.* U.S.D.A. Forest Service Northern Forest Expt. Sta. Gen. Tech. Rept. NE-13, Upper Darby, Pa.

Douglass, J. E., and W. T. Swank. 1976 Multiple use in southern Appalachian hardwoods—10-year case history. *XVI IUFRO World Congress,* Div. 1 Proc. pp. 425–36.

Douglass, J. E., and H. van Lear. (In Press) Prescribed burning and water quality of ephemeral streams in the Piedmont of South Carolina. *Forest Science.*

Dragoun, F. R., and L. L. Harrold. 1971. Flood hydrology of a small watershed. *Trans. American Soc. Agricultural Engineering* 14:1129–31.

Duldulao, A. 1981. The implications of forest occupancy management of natural resources conservation. *Philippine Development* 9(9):24–33.

Dyrness, C. T. 1967. Erodibility and erosion potential of forest watersheds. In *International Symposium on Forest Hydrology,* ed. W. E. Sopper and H. W. Lull, pp. 599–610. Oxford: Pergamon Press.

Eckholm, E. 1976. *Losing Ground.* New York: W. W. Norton.

Edwards, K. A., and J. R. Blackie. 1981. Results of the East African catchment experiments, 1958–1974. In *Tropical Agricultural Hydrology,* ed. R. Lal and E. W. Russell, pp. 163–88. New York: John Wiley and Sons.

Ekern, P. C. 1964. Direct interception of cloud water on Lanaihale, Hawaii. *Proc. Soil Science Soc. of America* 28:417–21.

El-Swaify, S. A., E. W. Dangler, and C. L. Armstrong. 1982. Soil erosion by water in the tropics. College of Tropical Agriculture and Human Resources, Univ. of Hawaii Research Extension Series 024, Honolulu.

European Environmental Bureau. 1982. The environmental importance of tropical moist forests. *Deforestation and Development Newsletter,* June 1982. pp. 1–7.

Evans, J. 1982. Plantation forestry in the tropics. Clarendon Press, Oxford.

Food and Agricultural Organization (FAO). 1979. 1977 Yearbook of Forest Products, 1966–1977, Rome.

Generalao, Maximo L. 1981. How to grow rattan. FORI How-To Series, No. 1, Forest Research Institute, College, Laguna, Philippines.

Gifford, G. F. 1978. Infiltrometer studies in rangeland plant communities of the Northern Territory. *Australian Rangeland* 1:142–149.

Gilmour, D. A. 1971. The effects of logging on streamflow and sedimentation in a north Queensland rainforest catchment. *Commonwealth Forestry Review* (Australia) 50:38–48.

Gilmour, D. A. 1977a. Logging and the environment with particular reference to soil and stream protection in tropical rainforest situations. In *Guidelines for Watershed Management.* FAO Conservation Guide 1, Rome, pp. 223–35.

Gilmour, D. A. 1977b. Effect of rainforest logging and clearing on water yield and quality in a high rainfall zone of northeast Queensland. Hydrology Symposium, Inst. of Engineers, Brisbane, pp. 156–60.

Gilmour, D. A., M. Bonell, and D. F. Sinclair. 1980 An investigation of storm drainage processes in a tropical rainforest catchment. Australian Water Resources Council Tech. Paper 56, Canberra.

Gilmour, D. A., D. S. Cassells, and M. Bonell. 1982. Hydrological research in the tropical rainforests of north Queensland: Some implications for land use management. *Proc. First National Symp. on Forest Hydrology*, Melbourne, pp. 145–52.

Gintings, A. N. 1981. Surface runoff and soil erosion on land covered by coffee plantation versus undisturbed natural forest in Sumberjaya, Lampung, Sumatra. M.S. Thesis, Graduate School, IPB, Bogor.

Golley, F., B. Hopkins, and F. Bernhard-Reversat. 1978. Decomposition and biogeochemical cycles. In *Tropical Forest Ecosystems: A state-of-knowledge report*, pp. 270–85. UNESCO/UNEP/FAO, Paris.

Gonggrijp, L. 1941. Het erosie onderzoek. *Tectona* 34/35:200–20.

Goodland, R. J. A., and H. S. Irwin. 1975. *Amazon Jungle: Green Hell to Red Desert?* Amsterdam: Elsevier.

Grainger, A. 1980. The state of the world's tropical forests. *The Ecologist* 10:6–54.

Graynoth, D. 1979. Effects of logging on stream environments and faunas in Nelson. *N.Z. Marine and Freshwater Research* 13:79–109.

Hamzah, A. 1978. Some observations on the effects of mechanical logging on regeneration, soil, and hydrological conditions in East Kalimantan. *Proc. Symposium on Long Term Effects of Logging in Southeast Asia*, BIO-TROP Spec. Publ. 3, Bogor, pp. 73–78.

Hamilton, L. S. 1976. *Tropical Rainforest Use and Preservation: A Study of Problems and Practices in Venezuela*. International Series No. 4, San Francisco: Sierra Club.

Hamilton, L. S., and M. Bonell. 1982. Country papers on status of watershed forest influence research in Southeast Asia and the Pacific. East-West Center Environment and Policy Institute Working Paper, Honolulu.

Harcombe, P. A. 1977. Nutrient accumulation by vegetation during the first year of recovery of a tropical forest ecosystem. In *Recovery and Restoration of Damaged Ecosystems*, ed. J. Cairns, K. Dickson, and E. Herricks, pp. 347–48. Virginia: University Press of Virginia.

Hardjono, H. W. 1980. The effect of permanent vegetation and its distribution on streamflow of three sub-watersheds in Central Java. Paper at Seminar on Hydrology and Watershed Management, Surakarta, 5 June 1980 (Unpublished).

Harr, R. D. 1980. Streamflow after patch logging in small drainages within the Bull Run municipal watershed, Oregon. U.S.D.A. Forest Service Pacific Northwest Forest and Range Expt. Sta. Research Paper P.N.W.-268, Portland, Or.

Hecht, S. B. 1980. Deforestation in the Amazon Basin: Magnitude, dynamics and soil resource effects. In *Where Have All the Flowers Gone? Deforestation in the Third World*, ed. V. H. Sutlive, N. Altshuler, and M. D. Zamora, pp. 61 – 108, Dept. Anthropology, Publ. 13. Williamsburg: College of William and Mary.

Helvey, J. D. 1967. Interception by eastern white pine. *Water Resources Research* 3:723 – 29.

Helvey, J. D. 1981. Flood frequency and culvert sizes needed for small watersheds in the central Appalachians. U.S.D.A. Forest Service Northeastern Forest Expt. Sta. Gen. Tech. Rept. NE-62, Upper Darby, Pa.

Helvey, J. D., and J. E. Douglass. 1971. Effects of some forest resource management alternatives on storm hydrograph characteristics in the southern Appalachians. Paper presented at IURFRO Congress, Gainesville, Fl. (Unpublished).

Hewlett, J. D. 1967. A hydrologic response map for the state of Georgia. *Water Resources Bull.* 3:4 – 20.

Hewlett, J. D. 1982. Forests and floods in the light of recent investigation. In *Proc. Canadian Hydrological Symp.* June 14 – 15, Fredericton, pp. 543 – 60.

Hewlett, J. D., G. B. Cunningham, and C. A. Troendle. 1977a. Predicting stormflow and peakflow from small basins in humid areas by the R-index method. *Water Resources Bull.* 13:231 – 53.

Hewlett, J. D., and J. E. Douglass. 1968. Blending forest uses. U.S.D.A. Forest Service Southeastern Forest Expt. Sta. Research Paper SE-37, Asheville, N.C.

Hewlett, J. D., J. C. Fortson, and B. G. Cunningham. 1977b. The effect of rainfall intensity on storm flow and peak discharge from forest land. *Water Resources Research* 13:259 – 66.

Hewlett, J. D., and J. D. Helvey. 1970. Effects of forest clearfelling on the storm hydrograph. *Water Resources Research* 6:768 – 82.

Hewlett, J. D., and A. R. Hibbert. 1967. Factors affecting the response of small watersheds to precipitation in humid areas. In *International Symposium on Forest Hydrology*, ed. W. E. Sopper and H. W. Lull, pp. 275 – 90. Oxford: Pergamon.

Hibbert, A. R. 1967. Forest treatment effects on water yield. In *International Symposium on Forest Hydrology*, ed. W. E. Sopper and H. W. Lull, pp. 527 – 43. Oxford: Pergamon.

Hibbert, A. R. 1969. Water yield changes after converting a forest catchment to grass. *Water Resources Research* 5:634 – 40.

Hibbert, A. R., and G. B. Cunningham. 1967. Streamflow data processing opportunities and application. In *International Symposium on Forest Hydrology*, ed. W. E. Sopper and H. W. Lull, pp. 725 – 36. Oxford: Pergamon.

Hofstad, O. 1978. Preliminary evaluation of the taunga system for combined wood and food production in Northeastern Tanzania. Record Div. of Forestry, Univ. of Dar es Salaam No. 2. *Forestry Abstracts* 41:4664.

161

Holmes, J. W., and E. B. Wronski. 1982. On the water harvest from afforested catchments. *Proc. First National Symposium on Forest Hydrology*, Melbourne, pp. 1–6.

Hoover, M. D. 1945. Careless skidding reduces benefits of forest cover to watershed protection. *Forestry* 43:765–66.

Hudson, N. W. 1971. *Soil Conservation*. Ithaca: Cornell Univ. Press.

Hughes, J. G., D. McClatchy, and J. A. Hayward. 1968. Cattle in South Island hill and high country. Tussock Mountain Lands Inst., Lincoln Coll., Christchurch.

Hunting Technical Services. 1971. Johor Tengah and Tanjung Penggerang regional masterplan. Hunting Technical Services, Ltd., Boreham Wood, England.

Ignatieff, V., and H. J. Page (eds.) 1958. *Efficient Use of Fertilizers*. FAO Agricultural Studies 43, Rome, pp. 160–63.

Isaac, L. A. 1946. Fog drip and rain interception in coastal forests. U.S.D.A. Forest Service, Pacific Northwest Forest and Range Expt. Sta. Research Note 34, Portland, Or.

Jordan, C. F. 1980. Nutrient leaching from agro-ecosystems in the Amazon Basin, and implications for recovery for the forest. In *Tropical Ecology and Development*, ed. J. I. Furtado, Part 1, pp. 553–59. Kuala Lumpur: Int. Soc. Tropical Ecology.

Jordan, C. F., and R. Herrera. 1981. Tropical rainforests: Are nutrients really critical? *Nature and Resources* 17(2):7–13.

Kammer, R., and Raj. 1979. Preliminary estimates of minimum flows in Varaciva Creek and the effect of afforestation on water resources. Fiji Public Works Department Tech. Note 79/1. Suva.

Kang, B. T., and R. Lal. 1981. Nutrient losses in water runoff from agricultural catchments. In *Tropical Agricultural Hydrology*, ed. R. Lal and E. W. Russell, pp. 153–61. New York: John Wiley and Sons.

Kartawinata, K. 1981. The environmental consequences of tree removal from the forest in Indonesia. In *Where Have All the Flowers Gone? Deforestation in the Third World*, Publ. 13 ed. V. H. Sutlive, N. Altshuler, and M. D. Zamora. pp. 191–214. Williamsburg: College of William and Mary.

Kellman, M. C. 1969. Some environmental components of shifting cultivation in upland Mindanao, *Tropical Geography* 28:40–56.

Kidd, W. J. Jr. 1963. Soil erosion control structures on skid trails. U.S.D.A. Forest Service Intermountain Forest and Range Expt. Sta. Research paper INT-1. Ogden, Vt.

Knight, P. J., and G. M. Will. 1977. A field lysimeter to study water movement and nutrient content in a pumice soil under *Pinus radiata* forest. II-deep seepage and nutrient leaching in the first 12 years of tree growth. *New Zealand Forest Science* 7:274–96.

Kunkle, S. H. (In Press). Forestry support for agriculture through watershed management, windbreaks, and other conservation actions. *Proc. Eighth World Forestry Congress, Jakarta* IUFRO.

Kunstadter, Peter, and E. C. Chapman. 1978. Problems of shifting cultivation and economic development in northern Thailand. In *Farmers in the Forest*, ed. Peter Kunstadter, E. C. Chapman, and Sanga Sabhasri, pp. 3 – 23. Honolulu: East-West Center.

Lal, R. 1979. Effects of cultural and harvesting practices on soil physical conditions. In *Soils Research in Agroforestry*, ed. H. O. Mongi and P. A. Huxley, pp. 327 – 51. Nairobi: Int. Council for Research in Agroforestry.

Lal, R. 1981. Deforestation of tropical rainforest and hydrologic problems. In *Tropical Agricultural Hydrology*, ed. R. Lal and E. W. Russell, pp. 131 – 40. New York: John Wiley and Sons.

Lal, R., and E. W. Russell (eds.). 1981. *Tropical Agricultural Hydrology—watershed management and land use*. New York: John Wiley and Son.

Langford, K. J. 1974. Changes in yield of water following a bush fire in a forest of *Eucalyptus regnans*. Melbourne and Metropolitan Board of Works Report MMBW-W-0003, Melbourne.

Lasser, T. 1955. Hacie de restauracion de la cuenca del Santo Domingo. *Revista Pecuaria* 23(242):11 – 12.

Lea, D. A. M. 1975. Human sustenance and the tropical forest. In *Ecological effect of increasing human activities on tropical and sub-tropical forest ecosystems*. pp. 83 – 102. Canberra: Australian UNESCO Comm. for Man and the Biosphere (MAB).

Likens, G. E., F. H. Bormann, N. M. Johnson, D. W. Fisher, and R. S. Pierce. 1970. Effects of forest cutting and herbicide treatment on nutrient budgets in the Hubbard Brook watershed ecosystem. *Ecol. Monographs* 40: 23 – 47.

Lim Suan, M. P. 1980. Technical feasibility and economic viability of selective logging in the Insular Lumber Company. Forest Research Inst. Annual Rept. College, Laguna, Philippines. pp. 142 – 43.

Low, K. S., and K. C. Goh. 1972. Water balance studies in Selangor, West Malaysia. *Tropical Geography* 35:60 – 66.

Low, K. S., and C. H. Leigh. 1972. Floods, soil erosion, and water quality in West Malaysia-adjustments to disruptions of natural systems. *Institution Engineers Malaysia* 14:14 – 19.

Lundgren, B. 1979. Research strategy for soils in agroforestry. In *Soils Research in Agroforestry*, ed. H. O. Mongi and P. A. Huxley, pp. 523 – 38. Nairobi: Int. Council for Research in Agroforestry, Nairobi.

McArthur, A. G. 1964. Streamflow characteristics of forested catchments. *Australian Forestry* 28:106 – 18.

McArthur, A. G., and N. P. Cheney. 1965. The effect of management practice on streamflow and sedimentation from forested catchments. *Inst. Engineers Australia* 37:417 – 25.

McCashion, J. S., and R. M. Rice. 1983. Erosion on logging roads in north-western California: how much is avoidable? *Forestry* 81:23–26.

McCauley, D. 1982. Soil erosion and land use patterns among upland farmers in the Cimanuk watershed of West Java, Indonesia. East-West Environment and Policy Institute Working Paper, Honolulu.

McDonald, D. C. 1955. Soil moisture and physical properties of a Westland "pakihi" soil in relation to deforestation. *N.Z. Science and Technology* 37:258–66.

McDonald, L. H. (ed.). 1982. *Agro-forestry in the African humid tropics.* Tokyo: United Nations University.

Masrur, A., and M. Hanif. 1972. A study of surface runoff and sediment release in a chir pine area. *Pakistan Forestry* 22:113–41.

Mathur, H. N., Rambabu, P. Joshie and B. Singh. 1976. Effect of clearfelling and reforestation on runoff and peak rates in small watersheds. *Indian Forester.* 102:219–26.

Megahan, W. F. 1976. Effects of forest cultural treatments on streamflow. In *Proc. Forest Acts Dilemma Symp.,* pp. 14–34. Missoula: University of Montana.

Megahan, W. F. 1977. Reducing erosional impacts of roads. In *Guidelines for Watershed Management.* FAO Conservation Guide 1, Rome, pp. 237–61.

Megahan, W. F. 1981. Nonpoint source pollution from forestry activities in the western United States: Results of recent research and research needs. In *U.S. Forestry and Water Quality: What Course in the 80's?* Proc. Water Pollution Control Federation Meeting, Washington, pp. 92–151.

Megahan, W. F., and W. J. Kidd. 1972. Effects of logging and logging roads on erosion and sediment deposition from steep terrain. *Forestry,* 70:136–41.

Melzer, A. D. 1962. A preliminary report on the Callide Valley investigation. Irrigation and Water Supply Commission, Queensland, Internal Report, Brisbane.

Michaelson, T. 1975. Observaciones de erosion en plantaciones de teca, *Tectona grandis.* Direccion General de Recursos Naturales Renovables, Servicio de Ordenacion de Cuencas, San Salvador.

Mitchell, A. and P. N. King. 1980. Land use and management of water supply catchments. Soil Conservation Authority of Victoria Reprint from Proc. Australian Agronomy Conf., Queensland Agric. Coll. Lawes.

Mosley, M. P. (In Press). The effect of a New Zealand beech forest canopy on the kinetic energy of water drops and on surface erosion. *Earth Surface Processes.*

Mott, J., B. J. Bridge, and W. Arndt. 1979. Soil seals in tropical tall grass pastures of northern Australia. *Australian Journal of Soil Research* 30:483–94.

Mueller-Dombois, D. 1973. A non-adapted vegetation interferes with water removal in a tropical rainforest area in Hawaii. *Tropical Ecology* 14: 1–18.

Murai, H. 1973. Soil conservation in grazing land. Japan Forest Technique Association. Forest Technique Extension Series No. 49, Tokyo.

Murai, H., Y. Iwasaki, and M. Ishii. 1975. Effects on hydrological conditions by the exchanging of ground cover from forest land to grassland. Association Internationale des Sciences Hydrologiques Symposium de Tokyo Publ. 117, pp. 457–64.

Nakano, H. 1967. Effect of changes of forest conditions on water yield, peak flow and direct runoff of small watersheds in Japan. In *International Symposium on Forest Hydrology*, ed. W. E. Sopper and H. W. Lull, pp. 551–64. Oxford: Pergamon.

Nakano, H. 1971. Effect on streamflow of forest cutting and change in regrowth on cut-over area. Bull. Govt. Forest Expt. Sta. 240, Tokyo.

Naprakob, B., P. Lapudomlers, and Y. Witchirjutipong. 1975. Sediment yield from shifting cultivation at Chiang Dao Watershed Research Station, Chiang Mai. Research Section, Watershed Management Division, Royal Thai Forest Dept., Bangkok, pp. 75–81.

New Zealand Forest Service. 1977. Management policy for New Zealand's indigenous state forests, Wellington.

Nye, P. H., and D. J. Greenland. 1960. The soil under shifting cultivation. Commonwealth Agricultural Bureau Tech. Comm. No. 51, Farnham Royal, England.

O'Loughlin, C. L. 1974. The effect of timber removal on the stability of forest soils. *Hydrology* 13:121–34.

O'Loughlin, C. L., and A. J. Pearce. 1976. Influence of cenozoic geology on mass movement and sediment yield response to forest removal, north Westland, New Zealand. *Bull. Int. Assoc. Engineering Geology* 14:41–48.

O'Loughlin, C. L., and A. J. Watson. 1979. Root wood strength deterioration in radiata pine after clearfelling. *N.Z. Forestry Science* 9:284–93.

O'Loughlin, C. L., L. K. Rowe, and A. J. Pearce. 1980. Sediment yield and water quality responses to clearfelling of evergreen mixed forests in western New Zealand. International Association of Hydrological Sciences Publ. 130, pp. 285–92.

Openshaw, K. 1974. Woodfuels in the developing world. *New Scientist*, January 31, p. 271–72.

Pearce, A. J. 1980. Water yield consequences of vegetation changes. In *Proceedings of Seminar on Land Use in Relation to Water Quality and Quantity*. Nelson Catchment Board Publication, Nelson, N.Z.

Pearce, A. J., and L. K. Rowe. 1979. Forest management effects on interception evaporation and water yield. *Hydrology (N.Z.)* 18: 73–87.

Pearce, A. J., L. K. Rowe, and C. L. O'Loughlin. 1980. Effects of clearfelling and slashburning on water yields and storm hydrographs in evergreen mixed forests, western New Zealand. International Association of Hydrological Sciences Publ. 130. pp. 119– 27.

Peh, C. H. 1978. Rates of sediment transport by surface wash in three forested areas of Peninsular Malaysia. Dept. of Geography, Univ. of Malaya Occ. Paper No. 3.

Peh, C. H. 1980. Runoff and sediment transport by overland flow under tropical rain forest conditions. *The Malaysian Forester* 43:56– 67.

Pereira, H. C. 1972. Influence of man on the hydrologic cycle: Guide to policies for the safe development of land and water resources. In *Studies and Trends of Research in Hydrology. 1965– 74*, pp. 31– 70. Paris: UNESESCO.

Pereira, H. C. 1973. *Land Use and Water Resources in Temperate and Tropical Climates*, London: Cambridge Univ. Press.

Pereira, C. 1979. Hydrological and soil conservation aspects of agroforestry. In *Soils Research in Agroforestry*, ed. H. O. Mongi and P. A. Huxley, pp. 315– 26. Nairobi: Int. Council for Research in Agroforestry, Nairobi.

Pereira, H. C., and P. H. Hosegood. 1962. Comparative water use of softwood plantations and bamboo forest. *Soil Science* 13:299– 314.

Queensland Department of Forestry. 1977. Research Report No. 1, Brisbane, pp. 72– 74.

Raeder-Roitzsch, J. E., and A. Masur. 1968. Some hydrologic relationships of natural vegetation in the chir pine belt of Pakistan. *Proc. First Pakistan Watershed Management Conference*, Pakistan Forest Institute, Peshawar, pp. 345– 60.

Reinhart, H. G., A. R. Eschner, and G. R. Trimble, Jr. 1963. Effects on streamflow of four forest practices, in the mountains of West Virginia. U.S. Forest Service Northeastern Forest Expt. Sta. Research Paper. NE1, Upper Darby, Pa.

Rice, R. M. 1977. Forest management to minimize landslide risk. In *Guidelines for Watershed Management*. FAO Conservation Guide 1, Rome, pp. 271– 87.

Rice, R. M. and P. A. Datzman. 1980. Erosion associated with cable and tractor logging in northwestern California. U.S.D.A. Forest Service, Pacific Southwest Forest and Range Expt. Sta. Unpublished Report. Berkeley.

Rice, R. M., and G. T. Foggin. 1971. Effect of high intensity storms on soil slippage on mountainous watersheds in southern California. *Water Resources Research* 7:1485– 96.

Rice, R. M., J. S. Rothacher, and W. F. Megahan. 1972. Erosional consequences of timber harvesting: An appraisal. *Proc. National Symposium Watersheds in Transition*, Fort Collins, Co. pp. 321– 29.

Rowe, P. B. 1941. Some factors of the hydrology of the Sierra Nevada foothills. *American Geophysical Union Trans.* 22:90– 100.

Ruslan, M., and S. Manan. 1980. The effect of skidding road on soil erosion and runoff in the forest concession of Pulan Laut, South Lakimantou, Indonesia. Paper at Seminar on Hydrology in Watershed Management, Sura Karta, (Unpublished).

Russell, E. W. 1981. Role of watershed management for arable land use in the tropics. In *Tropical Agricultural Hydrology*. ed. R. Lal and E. W. Russell, pp. 11– 16. New York: John Wiley and Sons.

Sajise, P. E. 1977. Regeneration of critical upland areas: An ecological imperative. Unpublished professorial lecture, University of the Philippines at Los Banos, Laguna, Philippines.

Salati, E. 1981. Precipitation and water recycling in tropical rain forests with special reference to the Amazon Basin. Unpublished position paper presented to workshop at Centro de Energia nuclear na Agricultura, Piracicaba, Sao Paulo, November 10– 13.

Salati, E., A. Dall'Olio, E. Matsui and J. R. Gat. 1979. Recycling of water in the Amazon Basin: an isotopic study. *Water Resources Research* 15:1250– 58.

Sanchez, P. A. 1979. Soil fertility and conservation considerations for agroforestry systems in the humid tropics of Latin America. In *Soils Research in Agroforestry*, ed. H. O. Mongi and P. A. Huxley, pp. 79– 124. Nairobi: Int. Council for Research in Agroforestry.

Sanchez, P. A. 1981. Soils of the humid tropics. In *Blowing in the Wind: Deforestation and Long-range Implications*, ed. V. H. Sutlive, N. Altshuler, and M. D. Zamora, pp. 347– 410. Studies in Third World Societies No. 14, Williamsburg: College of William and Mary.

Saplaco, S. 1981. Sediment yield from five ecosystems in a watershed at Mt. Makiling Forest. Upland Hydroecology Program (1977– 1980). Summary made for workshop, College, Laguna, Philippines.

Scott, G. A. J. 1974. Grassland formation in a tropical rainforest climate and its effect on the soil vegetation nutrient pools and nutrient cycles: A case study in the Gran Pajonal of Eastern Peru. Ph.D. thesis, Dept. Geography, University of Hawaii.

Shallow, P. G. 1956. River flow in the Cameron Highlands. Hydroelectric Tech. Memo. No. 3, Central Electricity Board, Kuala Lumpur.

Sharp, A. L., A. E. Gibbs and W. S. Owen. 1966. Development of a procedure for estimating the effects of land and watershed treatment on streamflow. U.S.D.A. Tech. Bull 1352, Washington.

Sharp, D., and T. Sharp. 1982. The desertification of Asia. *ASIA 2000* 1(4):40– 42.

Spears, John. 1982. Rehabilitating watersheds. *Finance and Development* 19(1):30– 33.

Swank, W. T., and J. E. Douglass. 1974. Streamflow greatly reduced by converting deciduous hardwood stands to pine. *Science* 185:857– 59.

Swank, W. T., and J. E. Douglass. 1977. Nutrient budgets for undisturbed and manipulated hardwood forest ecosystems in the mountains of

North Carolina. In *Watershed Research in Eastern North America: A workshop to compare results*, ed. David L. Correll, Vol. I, pp. 343–64. Edgewater, Md.: Smithsonian Institute.

Swank, W. T., and N. H. Miner. 1968. Conversion of hardwood-covered watersheds to white pine reduces water yield. *Water Resources Research* 4:947–54.

Swift, L. W., Jr., W. T. Swank, J. B. Mankin, R. J. Luxmoore, and R. A. Goldstein. 1975. Simulation of evapotranspiration and drainage from mature and clearcut deciduous forests and young pine plantation. *Water Resources Research* 11:667–73.

Tejwani, K. G. 1979. Soil fertility status, maintenance, and conservation for agroforestry systems on wasted lands in India. In *Soils Research in Agroforestry*, eds. H. O. Mongi and P. A. Huxley pp. 141–74. Nairobi: Int. Council for Research in Agroforestry.

Tennessee Valley Authority (TVA). 1962. Reforestation and erosion control influences upon the hydrology of the Pine Tree Branch Watershed, 1941 to 1960. TVA, Knoxville.

Teoh, T. S. 1973. Some effects of *Hevea* plantations on rainfall redistribution. *Proc. Symposium on Biological Resources and National Development*, Kuala Lumpur, pp. 73–83.

Toebes, C., and K. S. Goh. 1975. Notes on some hydrological effects of land use change in Peninsular Malaysia. *Water Resources and National Development*, Kuala Lumpur, pp. 73–83.

Trustrum, N. A., M. G. Lambert and V. J. Thomas. (In press). The impact of soil slip erosion on hill country pasture production in New Zealand. *Proc. Second Int. Conference on Soil Erosion and Conservation*, January 1983, Honolulu.

Tsukamoto, Y. 1975. Effect of forest litters on runoff cycle in a small experimental watershed. Publication 117 de l'Association Internationale des Sciences Hydrologiques, Symposium de Tokyo, pp. 487–95.

Tsukamoto, Y., and K. Kimura. 1976. An example of erosion which occured on forest fired land. Japan Forestry Soc. Trans. 87th Mtg., pp. 325–37.

UNESCO. 1969. Draft for the report of the working group to the mid-decade conference. Working Group on Influence of Man on the Hydrologic Cycle.

U.S. Interagency Task Force on Tropical Forests. 1980. The world's tropical forests: A policy, strategy and program for the United States. Dept. of State Publ. 9117, Washington.

Van Lill, W. S., F. J. Kruger, and D. B. VanWyk. 1980. The effect of afforestation with *Eucalyptus grandis* (Hill ex maiden) and *Pinus patula* (Schlect. et Cham.) on streamflow from experimental catchments at Mokobulaan, Transvaal. *Hydrology* 48:107–18.

Veracion, V. P., and A. C. B. Lopez. 1975. Rainfall interception in a thinned

Benguet pine forest stand. *Sylvatrop: Philippines Forest Research* 1:128–34.

Vergara, N. T. (ed.). 1982. New directions in agroforestry: The potential of tropical legume trees. Improving agroforestry in the Asia-Pacific tropics. Honolulu: East-West Center Environment and Policy Institute.

Vogelmann, H. W. 1973. Fog precipitation in the cloud forests of Eastern Mexico. *Bioscience* 23:96– 100.

Wadsworth, F. 1978. Deforestation—death to the Panama Canal. *Proc. U.S. Strategy Conference on Tropical Deforestation.* U.S. Dept. of State and U.S. Agency for International Development, Washington. pp. 22– 24.

Watters, R. F. 1971. Shifting cultivation in Latin America. FAO Forestry Development Paper 17, Rome.

Whitmore, J. L. 1981. Plantations versus other land use options in Latin America. *Proc. XVII IUFRO World Congress,* Japan, Division 1: pp. 448–62. Vienna: IUFRO Secretariat.

Wicht, C. C. 1949. Forestry and water supplies in South Africa Dept. Agric. South Africa Bull. 58, Cape Town.

Wiersum, K. F. 1981. Outline of the agroforestry concept. In *Viewpoints on Agroforestry,* ed. K. F. Wiersum. pp. 1– 29. Wageningen: Hinkeloord, Agricultural University.

Williams, J., and L. S. Hamilton. 1982. Watershed forest influences in the tropics and subtropics: A selected, annotated bibliography. Honolulu: East-West Center Environment and Policy Institute.

Wood, H. B., R. A. Merriam, and I. H. Schubert. 1969. Vegetation recovering little erosion on Hanalei watershed after fire. U.S.D.A. Forest Service Pacific Southwest Forest Expt. Sta. Research Note PSW-191, Berkeley.

Working Group on the Influence of Man on the Hydrologic Cycle. 1972. Influence of man on the hydrologic cycle: Guide to policies for the safe development of land and water resources. In *Status and Trends of Research in Hydrology,* pp. 31– 70. Paris: UNESCO.

WWF/IUCN. 1982. Tropical forest campaign. World Wildlife Fund booklet. Gland, Switzerland.

Zadroga, F. 1981. The hydrological importance of a montane cloud forest area of Costa Rica. In *Tropical Agricultural Hydrology,* ed. R. Lal and F. W. Russell, pp. 59– 73. New York: John Wiley and Sons.